To Uncle John.

Wishing you a very happy 86th Birthday.

Jack, Marina

The Believers Hymn Book Companion

by
Harold S. Paisley

AUGUST 1989
Published by
GOSPEL TRACT PUBLICATIONS
411 Hillington Road, Glasgow G52 4BL, Scotland

ISBN 0 948417 54 4

Copyright © 1989
GOSPEL TRACT PUBLICATIONS

Printed by
GOSPEL TRACT PUBLICATIONS
411 Hillington Road, Glasgow G52 4BL, Scotland

List of Authors and Contents

Alexander, C.F. 8
Alystyne, F. van 10
Anonymous Hymn
   Writers 12
Auber, H. 14

Baker, H.W. 16
Bakewell, J. 18
Bancroft C.L. 20
Barnard, S. 22
Barton, B. 24
Barton, W. 26
Beattie, D.J. 28
Beaumont, J. 30
Bennett, H. 32
Bennett, L.A. 34
Bennett, W.H. 36
Bernard, C.V. 38
Bernstein, C.A. 40
Berridge, J. 42
Bevan, E.F. 44
Bickersteth, E. 46
Bickersteth, E.H. 48
Binney, T. 50
Blane, W. 52
Bliss, P.P. 54
Bode, J.E. 56
Boden, J. 58
Bonar, H. 60
Boswell, R. 62
Bottome, F. 64
Bridges, M. 66
Bubier G.B. 68
Burder, G. 70
Burlingham, H.K. . . . 72

Cameron, W. 74
Carson, M.L. 76
Carter, M. 78

Cennick, J. 80
Champney,
   H.D'A. 82
Chapman, R.C. 84
Charles, E.R. 86
Clausnitzer, T. 88
Clephane, E.C. 90
Codner, E. 92
Condor, J. 94
Cousin, A.R. 96
Cowper, W. 98
Crawford, E.M. . . . 100
Crewdson, J. 102
Cushing, W.O. 104

Dana, M.S.B. 106
Darby, J.N. 108
Dark, E. 110
Davies, S. 112
Deck, J.G. 114
Denny, Sir E. 116
Deszler, W.C. 118
De Fleury, M. 120
Dickinson, W. 122
Doddridge, P. 124

East, J. 126
Elders, K.H. 128
Ellerton, J. 130
Elliott, C. 132
Elwin, J.F. 134
Evans, J.H. 136

Faber, F.W. 138
Farningham, M. . . . 140
Fawcett, J. 142
Featherstone,
   W.R. 144
Flint, A.J. 146

Francis, S.T. 148
Fraser, G.W. 150
Furlong, G. 152

Gandy, S.W. 154
Gerhardt, P. 156
Gilbert, A.T. 158
Gilmour, J.H. 160
Goodman, G. 162
Grant, Sir R. 164
Grimley, E. 166
Guinness, H.G. 168
Gurney, J.H. 170

Hall, J.E. 172
Hammond, E.P. . . . 174
Hammond, W. 176
Hart, J. 178
Havergal, F.R. 180
Haweis, T. 182
Hawker, R. 184
Heber, R. 186
Hewitt, E.E. 188
Hoare, M.J. 190
Homburg, E.C. 192
Hope, H.J.McC. . . . 194
Hoskins, J. 196
Hull, A.M. 198
Hurditch, C.R. 200
Hutton, J. 202

Iverson, W.A. 204

Jekel, G. 206

Keene, R. 208
Kelly, T. 210
Ken, T. 212
Kent, J. 214

3

Kingsbury, H. 216	Perronet, E. 292	Thompson, B. 372
Kuster, S.C.G. 218	Peters, M 294	Thompson, C. 374
	Phelps, S.D. 296	Tomkins, W.N. . . . 376
Lathbury, M.A. . . . 220	Pierson, A.T. 298	Toplady, M.A. 378
Lavater, J.C. 222	Piggott, J.S. 300	Tregelles, S.P. 380
Leeson, J.E. 224	Price, J. 302	Trench, G.F. 382
Lloyd, W.F. 226		Trench, J.A. 384
Logan, J. 228	Quine, E.C. 304	Turner, H.L. 386
Lowry, R. 230		
Lyte, H.F. 232	Ramsey, B.M. 306	Wakefield, E. 388
	Rawson, G. 308	Walker, M.J.D. 390
Madan, M. 234	Reid, W. 310	Waring, A.L. 392
Marriott, J. 236	Reynolds, T.H. 312	Waring, S.M. 394
Mason, J. 238	Robinson, R. 314	Warner, A.B. 396
Matheson, G. 240	Rossier, Dr. H.L. . . 316	Watts, I. 398
Maxwell, M.E. 242	Rous, F. 318	Wellesley, C.A. . . . 400
Medley, S. 244	Russell, D. 320	Wesley, C. 402
Midlane, A. 246	Rutherford, A.J. . . . 322	Wesley, J. 404
Miln, E.M. 248	Ryland, I. 324	Whately, M. 406
McKay, A.B. 250		Whatley, R 408
Monod, T. 252	Scriven, J.M. 326	Whitfield, F. 410
Monsell, J.S.B. 254	Shekleton, M. 328	Whittier, J.G. 412
Montgomery, J. . . . 256	Shirley, Sir W. 330	Whittingham,
Moore, T. 258	Sloan, W.G. 332	W. 414
Morison, J. 260	Small, J.G. 334	Whittle, D.W. 416
Morshead, W. 262	Smith, J.D. 336	Wigram, F.T. 418
Moule, H.C.G. 264	Smith, W.C. 338	Wilkinson, K.B. . . . 420
Mote, E. 266	Spafford, H.G. 340	Williams, W. 422
Mullen, B. 268	Spurgeon, C.H. 342	Willis, E.H. 424
Macalister,	Steele, A. 344	Winkworth, C. 426
R.A.S. 270	Stennett, J. 346	Withy, J. 428
McCheyne, R.M. . . 272	Stennett, S. 348	Wordsworth, C. . . . 430
McGranahan, J. . . . 274	Sternhold, T. 350	
Mackay, W.P 276	Stewart, A. 352	Yerbury, W. 432
	Stites, E.P. 354	
Neander, J. 278	Stock, S.G. 356	Zinzendorf,
Nelson, D. 280	Stockton, J.H. 358	N.L.C. 434
	Stone, S.J. 360	
Newton, J. 282	Stowell, H. 362	Selected
Noel, C.M. 284	Swain, J. 364	Bibliography 437
		General Reference
Olivers, T. 286	Taylor, T.R. 366	Works 438
	Tersteegen, G. 368	
Paget, C. 288	Theodulf of	Index of First
Palmer, R. 290	Orleans 370	Lines 439

Preface

The first edition of the Believers Hymn Book was published in 1888 and contained 361 hymns. A further useful supplement was added in 1959. There are over 200 writers concerning whom we have been able to research some information. In about 20 cases the availability of record is limited, and 27 other writers are anonymous.

The writers represent all walks of life, centuries of time, and various religious backgrounds. These men and women placed great value upon the Person, Work and Offices of the Lord Jesus Christ. Many of their hymns also reflect experiences of Christian life and service, an expectation of the return of the Saviour for His Church, and His final reign as King of Kings.

The purpose of this book is to acquaint the users of the Hymn Book, generally used in assemblies of the Lord's people, with information concerning the occasion of writing, and brief accounts of the authors.

The researching of the material has been a labour of love, covering a number of years, and necessitating the reading of many books on this wonderful and fascinating study of Hymnody.

It is hoped that a greater appreciation of the value of these precious hymns may produce fuller worship of the Father, increased devotion to the Son, our Lord and Saviour Jesus Christ, and a sweeter note of song in the power of the Holy Spirit, in anticipation of that glad time when all the redeemed will join in the everlasting song around the once-slain Lamb, in the eternal Glory.

It is of great personal interest to me that John Cennick wrote: "Brethren, let us join to bless Jesus Christ, our joy and peace" in the village of Gracehill, Northern Ireland. James Montgomery also wrote many of his beautiful hymns there, and planted a tree still growing in the village square. For it was in Gracehill that I first met my wife, who grew up in the village, and who has been a great help to me in writing this book, as in all my Christian ministry over many years.

Harold S. Paisley
Toronto, Canada　　　　　　　　　　　　November 12, 1988.

Three writers about whom we have no available information. Their compositions are exceedingly valuable and spiritual.

1. Carruthers, Alexander. (1860-1930).
   We bless Thee, God and Father 460

2. Costello, E. (c. 1920).
   Abide in me, my Saviour 362

3. C.A.H.
   The cloudless day is nearing...................... 262

CECIL FRANCES ALEXANDER

Alexander, Cecil Frances, nee Humphreys (Wicklow, Ireland, 1818—Londonderry, Ireland, Oct. 12, 1895).

Mrs Alexander was the daughter of Major Humphreys of the Royal Marines. She was a woman of great attractiveness in spite of her poor eyesight and excessive shyness. In 1850 she married Dr. William Alexander, who became Anglican Primate of Ireland.

In 1846 she published "Hymns for Children" specially for Sunday Schools. Its purpose was to teach the young the great truths of the Apostles' Creed. This collection, which had over 100 publications, was at once recognised as a work of great value. Some of these are included in most hymn books today. Two are in "The Believers Hymn Book." (398, 455)
Other hymns of note are:
"Once in Royal David's City" and
"All things bright and beautiful."

Mrs Alexander also wrote a number of poems. "The Burial of Moses" was declared by Lord Tennyson to be the finest sacred lyric in any language. He said he wished he had been the writer.

THE GREEN HILL

Hymn 455   Tune: *Horsley* C.M.

There is a green hill far away,
   Without a city wall,
Where the dear Lord was crucified,
   Who died to save us all.

We may not know, we cannot tell
   What pains He had to bear;
But we believe it was for us
   He hung and suffered there.

There was no other good enough
   To pay the price of sin;
He only could unlock the gate
   Of Heaven, and let us in.

JESUS CALLS US O'ER THE TUMULT
Hymn 398   Tune: *Galilee* 8.7.8.7.

Jesus calls us o'er the tumult
   Of our life's wild restless sea,
Day by day, His sweet voice soundeth
   Saying, Christian, follow Me.

As of old, apostles heard it
   By the Galilean lake,
Turned from home and toil and kindred,
   Leaving all for His dear sake.

CECIL FRANCES ALEXANDER

FRANCES JANE VAN ALYSTYNE

Alystyne, Frances van [Fanny J Crosby] (Southeast, New York, U.S.A. March 24 1820—Feb 12 1915. Bridgeport, Conn. U.S.A.).

Mrs Frances Jane van Alystyne is better known by her maiden name of Fanny Crosby. She lost her eyesight when six weeks old by the application of a wrong medication to her eyes. She was educated at the New York City Institute for the Blind. Afterwards she became a teacher of the blind in the Institute. In 1858 she married Alexander Van Alystyne, a blind musician.

Her first verses were published when she was eight years old, but she did not write hymns until after her conversion when she was in her forty fifth year.

She is said to have written over 8,000 hymns, which were published under 216 *nom de plume*, as well as in her maiden and married names. Sixty of her hymns are still in popular use. In one hymn (244 Believers Hymn Book) she expressed her devotion to the Lord Jesus in beautiful words:
Let me love Thee more and more,
Till this fleeting, fleeting life is o'er;
Till my soul is lost in love
In a brighter, brighter world above.

At the age of 95 she entered into that brighter world above.

CONSECRATION

Hymn 329 Tune: *Nearness*

I am Thine, O Lord! I have heard Thy voice,
   And it told Thy love to me;
But I long to rise in the arms of faith,
   And be closer drawn to Thee.

Draw me nearer, nearer Blessèd Lord,
   To the cross where Thou hast died,
Draw me nearer, nearer, nearer Blessèd Lord,
   To Thy precious, wounded side.

Consecrate me now to Thy service, Lord
   By the power of grace Divine;
Let my soul look up with a stedfast hope,
   And my will be lost in Thine.

Praise Him, Praise Him, Jesus our Blessed Redeemer 226
Safe in the arms of Jesus, safe on His gentle breast....... 243
Saviour more than Life to me.......................... 244
Take the world but give me Jesus, all its joys
   are but a name 259
Thou, my everlasting portion 294
Tis the blessèd hour of prayer 302
All the way my Saviour leads me...................... 364
Mine eyes are unto Thee 417
   F.J.M. (*nom de plume*)
Our great Redeemer Liveth............................ 437
   Fanny Hope (*nom de plume*)

FRANCES JANE VAN ALYSTYNE

ANONYMOUS HYMN WRITERS

Anonymous Hymn Writers—twenty seven hymns are included in the Believers Hymn Book with no writers identified.

These hymns have outstanding merit, expressing the love of the Saviour, our Lord Jesus Christ. Most of them have been used often in the gatherings of saints to "break bread" and worship the Father. Many of them anticipate the coming again of the Lord Jesus.

There is a day coming when all the redeemed shall meet and know those never seen or known before, including those whose hymns we have sung with joy and praise.

BEHOLD A SPOTLESS VICTIM DIES

Hymn 16   Tune: *Sidon* C.M.

Lord Jesus! Thou, and none beside,
Its bitterness could know,
Nor other tell Thy joy's full tide
That from that cup shall flow.

Christ the Lord is risen 37
Hark 'tis the watchman's cry 64
Here o'er the earth 72
How bright that blessed Hope 76
I am a stranger here 82
Joy, Joy, Joy 117
Lord Jesus my Saviour 133
Lord Jesus, Thou who only art 140
My Redeemer—O what beauties 159
My tongue shall spread 163
O Christian awake 177
Our Father! O what gracious ways 219
Our Father! we would worship 220
Praise Thy Saviour, O my soul 230
Rejoice ye saints 240
Son of God 'twas love that made Thee 250
Sweet are the seasons 253
The sorrows of the daily life 281
Though often here we'er weary 292
We come our gracious Father 311
We love to sing 312
Hark hark, hear the glad tidings 327
I will never, never leave thee 330
With steady pace the pilgrim moves 331
Is it Thy will that I should be 340

UNKNOWN HYMN WRITERS

HARRIOTT AUBER

Auber, Harriott (London, England, Oct. 4 1773—Jan. 20 1862, Hoddesdon, Herts, England).

Harriott Auber was the great grand-daughter of the well known Huguenot, Pierre Auber, of Normandy, France, who escaped to England as a refugee in 1685.

Most of her life was spent in the quiet village of Hoddesdon. She first published hymns in her book "The spirit of the Psalms" in 1829. Her best known hymn, which is included in the Believers Hymn Book is:

"Our blest Redeemer, ere He breathed
His tender last farewell"

This beautiful hymn portrays the gracious ministry of the Lord Jesus in the Upper Room (John 14-16) and especially His promise of the coming of the Person of the Holy Spirit.

The story is told that as she meditated upon this portion of the Word of God the hymn began to form in her mind. Neither pen nor paper were handy, but she was sitting near the window, so with her diamond ring she wrote the first verse on the window pane. The words remained for many years, but after the death of Miss Auber, the pane was removed by a thief, who was never discovered.

THE COMFORTER

Hymn 436   Tune: *St. Cuthbert* 8.6.8.4.

Our blest Redeemer, ere He breathed
  His tender last farewell,
A Guide, a Comforter bequeathed
  With us to dwell.

He came sweet influence to impart,
  A gracious, willing guest,
While He can find one humble heart
  Wherein to rest.

And His that gentle voice we hear,
  Soft as the breath of even,
That checks each fault, that calms each fear,
  And speaks of heaven.

And every virtue we possess,
  And every victory won,
And every thought of holiness
  Are His alone.

Spirit of purity and grace,
  Our weakness, pitying see;
O make our hearts, Thy dwelling place,
  Worthy of Thee.

HARRIOTT AUBER

SIR HENRY WILLIAMS BAKER

Baker, Henry Williams (London, England May 27, 1821— Monkland England Feb. 12, 1877).

Sir Henry Williams Baker, Baronet, was the son of a Vice-Admiral. He was a graduate of Trinity College, Cambridge.

Sir Henry W. Baker is a famous name in hymnody. He edited "Hymns Ancient and Modern."

One of his finest hymns: "The King of Love my Shepherd is," is a delightful rendering of Psalm 23, and is included in The Believers Hymn Book. This hymn is found in almost every hymnal in the English language.

Sir Henry passed home to be with Christ at the age of fifty six. As he was dying his last words were those of the third verse of his famous hymn:

"Perverse and foolish oft I strayed,
But yet in love He sought me,
And on His shoulder gently laid,
And home rejoicing brought me."

THE KING OF LOVE

Hymn 451   June: *St. Columba.* 8.7.8.7.

The King of love my Shepherd is,
  Whose goodness faileth never;
I nothing lack if I am His
  And He is mine for ever.

Where streams of living water flow
  My ransomed soul He leadeth,
And where the verdant pastures grow
  With food celestial feedeth.

Perverse and foolish oft I strayed,
  But yet in love He sought me,
And on His shoulder gently laid,
  And home rejoicing brought me.

In death's dark vale I fear no ill
  With Thee, dear Lord, beside me;
Thy rod and staff my comfort still,
  Thy cross before to guide me.

Thou spread'st a table in my sight,
  Thy unction grace bestoweth;
And O what transport of delight
  From Thy pure chalice floweth.

And so through all the length of days
  Thy goodness faileth never;
Good Shepherd, may I sing Thy praise
  Within Thy house for ever.

Lord, Thy word abideth, and our footsteps guideth 412

SIR HENRY WILLIAMS BAKER

JOHN BAKEWELL

Bakewell John (Brailsford, England 1721— Lewisham, England, 1819).

John Bakewell was an earnest evangelist with the Wesleys, and continued preaching the Gospel faithfully until over ninety years of age. He went to be with the Lord in his ninety ninth year. His one and only known contribution to hymnody is a hymn of worship and devotion to Christ.

The hymn is included in the Believers Hymn Book:
> "Hail, Thou once despisèd Jesus!
> Hail, Thou still rejected King!"

On the tombstone of John Bakewell in City Rd. Cemetry, London (near to John Wesley's grave) appears the following inscription:

> "John Bakewell departed this life March 18, 1819 aged 98.
> He adorned the doctrine of God our Saviour eighty years.
> He preached the Gospel seventy years.
> The memory of the just is blessed. Proverbs 10:7."

HAIL THOU ONCE DESPISÈD JESUS

Hymn 61   Tune: *Bethany* 8.7.8.7.D.

Hail, Thou once despisèd Jesus!
   Hail, Thou still rejected King!
Thou didst suffer to release us,
   Thou didst free salvation bring;
Through Thy death and resurrection,
   Bearer of our sin and shame!
We enjoy divine protection,
   Life and glory through Thy name.

Paschal Lamb, by God appointed,
   All our sins on Thee were laid;
By our Father's love anointed
   Thou hast full atonement made:
All who trust Thee are forgiven
   Through the virtue of Thy blood;
Rent in Thee the vail of heaven,
   Grace shines forth to man from God.

Saviour, hail! amid the glory,
   Where for us Thou dost abide;
We, by faith, do now adore Thee,
   Seated at Thy Father's side.
There, for us Thou now art pleading,
   While Thou dost our place prepare;
For Thy saints still interceding
   Till in glory we appear.

Worship, honour, praise, and blessing,
   Thou shalt then from all receive;
Loudest praises, without ceasing,
   All that earth or heaven can give:
In that day Thy saints will meet Thee,
   Welcome Thee with grateful song;
Joyful hearts will ever greet Thee,
   Source of joy to all the throng.

JOHN BAKEWELL

CHARITIE LEE BANCROFT

Bancroft Charitie Lee *nee* Smith (Dublin, Ireland 1841—Dublin 1923).

Charitie Lee Smith was the daughter of Dr. Sidney Smith, Drumreagh, Co. Tyrone, Northern Ireland. She married Arthur Bancroft in 1869. Mrs Bancroft expressed her conversion in the words of her well known hymn:

"Because the sinless Saviour died
My sinful soul is counted free;
For God, the Just, is satisfied
To look on Him and pardon me."

In 1867 her hymns were published in a small volume entitled *Within the Veil*. From this collection two hymns were selected for the Believers Hymn Book.

O FOR THE ROBES OF WHITENESS

Hymn 193   Tune: *Malabar* 7.6.7.6. D.

O for the robes of whiteness,
O for the tearless eyes;
O for the glorious brightness
Of the unclouded skies!
O for the no more weeping
Within the land of love;
The endless joy of keeping
The bridal feast above!

O Christ! Thou King of Glory,
I soon shall dwell with Thee!
I soon shall sing the story
Of Thy great love to me!
Meanwhile my soul would enter
E'en now before Thy throne,
That all my love might centre
On Thee, and Thee alone.

Before the Throne of God above 15

CHARITIE LEE BANCROFT

SAMUEL BARNARD

Barnard Samuel. Very little is known of this servant of Christ, who was a preacher of the gospel in the early part of the 19th century.

He wrote a number of hymns found in:
Spiritual Songs of Zion's Pilgrims.

The only one of his hymns still used is included in the Believers Hymn Book, namely:
"Jehovah is our Strength"

Each verse expresses one of the Glorious Titles of Christ.
The Lord our Refuge is—verse 2
The Lord our Portion is—verse 3
The Lord our Shepherd is—verse 4.

JEHOVAH IS OUR STRENGTH

Hymn 108   Tune: *Old 148th* 6.6.6.6.8.8.

Jehovah is our strength,
   And He shall be our song;
We shall o'ercome at length
   Although our foes be strong:
In vain then Satan doth oppose,
For God is stronger than His foes.

The Lord our refuge is,
   And ever will remain;
Since He hath made us His
   He will our cause maintain:
In vain our enemies oppose,
For God is stronger than His foes.

The Lord our portion is;
   What can we wish for more?
As long as we are His
   We never can be poor:
In vain do earth and hell oppose,
For God is stronger than His foes.

The Lord our Shepherd is;
   He knows our ev'ry need;
And since we now are His,
   His care our souls will feed:
In vain do sin and death oppose,
For God is stronger than His foes.

SAMUEL BARNARD

BERNARD BARTON

Barton Bernard (London, England Jan. 31, 1784— Woodbridge, England, Feb. 19, 1849).

Bernard Barton was known as England's "Quaker Poet".

Born in London, but grew up in Carlisle, he worked in his father's cotton manufacturing business. Later he and his brother worked together as coal merchants. Following the death of his wife, within one year of marriage, he came to the personal knowledge of Christ as his Saviour through the reading of the Word of God. He later wrote the well known hymn:

"Walk in the light, so shalt thou know
That fellowship of love
His Spirit only can bestow,
Who reigns in light above."

Barton wrote twenty hymns and also a number of fine poems. His poetical ability attracted the attention of Lord Byron. The English government granted him a State pension in his closing years for his contribution to English literature.

WALK IN THE LIGHT

Hymn 309   Tune: *Waveney* C.M.

Walk in the light, o'er sin abhorred
  Thou shalt the victory gain;
The blood of Jesus Christ Thy Lord
  Cleanseth from every stain.

Walk in the light, and thou shalt find
  Thy heart made truly His,
Who dwells in cloudless light enshrined,
  In whom no darkness is.

Walk in the light, and e'en the tomb
  No fearful shade shall wear;
Glory shall chase away the gloom,
  For Christ hath conquered there.

Walk in the light, and thine shall be
  A path, though thorny, bright;
For God, by grace, shall dwell in thee,
  And God Himself is light.

BERNARD BARTON

WILLIAM BARTON

Barton William (Leicester, England, 1603—Leicester, 1678).

William Barton was a minister of the Church of England in St. Martins of Leicester, over 300 years ago.

Barton was a man of devotion to the Lord and was a student of the Scriptures. He authored one of the earliest collection of hymns, as distinct from the Psalms.

Barton's metrical renderings of the *Te Deum* is a classic of English literature.

His best known work today is his hymn based upon the "King of Glory" as presented in the twenty-fourth Psalm.

YE GATES, LIFT UP YOUR HEADS ON HIGH

Hymn 463   Tune: *St. George's* D.C.M.

Ye gates, lift up your heads on high;
  Ye doors that last for aye
Be lifted up, that so the King
  Of glory enter may:
But who of glory is the King?
  The mighty Lord is this;
Ev'n that same Lord that great in might
  And strong in battle is.

Ye gates, lift up your heads; ye doors,
  Doors that do last for aye,
Be lifted up, that so the King
  Of glory enter may:
But who is He that is the King
  Of glory? who is this?
The Lord of hosts, and none but He,
  The King of glory is.

  Hallelujah! Hallelujah!
  Hallelujah! Hallelujah!
  Amen, Amen, Amen.

WILLIAM BARTON

DAVID JOHNSTONE BEATTIE

Beattie, David Johnstone (Langholm, Scotland, 1881— Carlisle, England, 2 July 1964).

David Beattie was saved in boyhood. He was in fellowship with the assembly of Christians meeting in Hebron Hall, Carlisle, for 65 years. He had a great interest in every facet of assembly life. He had a special concern for the spread of the Gospel, and supported the Cumberland and Westmoreland Tent work for many years.

Beattie was a keen research student in hymnology, and wrote two valuable and informative books on the subject:

The Romance of Sacred Song. and *Stories and Sketches of our Hymns and their Writers.*

He also wrote a number of hymns. His best known being: "Assembled Lord at Thy behest". This spiritual song is very appropriate when saints are gathered to remember the Lord.

Beattie's *History of the Brethren* is a very interesting record of the recovery of the Truth.

ASSEMBLED, LORD, AT THY BEHEST

Hymn 367   Tune: *Martyrdom* C.M.

Assembled, Lord, at Thy behest,
　We wait Thy voice to hear;
O come and bless this hallowed feast—
　In spirit now draw near.

Draw near, yea, linger in our midst;
　Thy waiting saints inspire
With thoughts of Thine unfailing love;
　Grant this our soul's desire.

Such love! surpassing human thought,
　That Thou, blest Lamb of God,
Should'st bear sin's curse, and interpose
　Thine own atoning blood.

With hearts adoring thus we view
　Thy table fitly spread;
Love's sweet memorial feast to Thee,
　Our risen, glorious Head.

O help us, Lord, while gathered here,
　That we none else may see;
Keep Thou our thoughts graced with Thy love,
　And wholly stayed on Thee.

DAVID JOHNSTONE BEATTIE

JOHN BEAUMONT

Beaumont John. (Went to be with Christ in 1879 from Ireland).

Very little information is available concerning John Beaumont.

He was one of the servants of God associated with J.N. Darby, A.N. Groves and J.G. Bellett, in the early days of the brethren movement in Ireland. He was a very able student of the Scriptures and preached the Gospel in many parts of Ireland and Europe during the latter part of his life.

We only know of one hymn which he wrote, but it expresses the love for the Saviour that moved the writer.

MY SHEPHERD IS THE LAMB

Hymn 156   Tune: *Zurich* S.M.

My Shepherd is the Lamb,
  The living Lord who died;
With all things good I ever am
  By Him in love supplied.

He richly feeds my soul
  With blessings from above,
And leads me where the rivers roll
  Of everlasting love.

His love so full, so free,
  Anoints my head with oil;
Goodness and mercy follow me,
  Fruit of His grief and toil.

When faith and hope shall cease,
  And love abides alone,
I then shall see Him face to face,
  And know as I am known.

JOHN BEAUMONT

HENRY BENNETT

Bennett Henry (Lyme Regis, England, April 18, 1813—Islington, England, Nov. 12, 1868).

Henry Bennett was led to personal faith in Christ when very young. He began early to write hymns. These were published as follows:

Hymns by H.B. this contained 25 hymns.

Hymns by Henry Bennett this contained 32 hymns.

From these editions of his hymns two are still in extensive use:

"I have a home above". and "Cling to the Mighty One".

His faith in Christ is expressed in the well known and often quoted verse:

"The Saviour's precious blood
 Has made our title sure:
He passed through death's dark raging flood
 To make our rest secure."

I HAVE A HOME ABOVE

Hymn 89   Tune: *Franconia* S.M.

I have a home above
From sin and sorrow free;
A mansion which eternal love
Designed and formed for me.

My Father's gracious hand
Has built this blest abode;
From everlasting it was planned
My dwelling-place with God.

Loved ones are gone before
Whose pilgrim days are done;
I soon shall greet them on that shore
Where partings are unknown.

But more than all, I long
His glories to behold,
Whose smile fills all the radiant throng
With ecstasy untold.

That bright, yet tender smile,
My sweetest welcome there,
Shall cheer me through the "little while"
I tarry for Him here.

Thy love, most gracious Lord,
My joy and strength shall be,
Till Thou shalt speak the gladd'ning word
That bids me rise to Thee.

And then, through endless days
Where all Thy glories shine,
In happier, holier strains I'll praise
The grace that made me Thine.

Cling to the mighty One............................... 36

HENRY BENNETT

LUCY ANN BENNETT

Bennett, Lucy Ann (England 1880—1927).
 Only one hymn is found written by Lucy Ann Bennett, but it shows in very spiritual language her faith and hope in the Lord Jesus Christ.

I AM THE LORD'S

Hymn 394   Tune: *Raynolds...Mendelssohn*

I am the Lord's! O joy beyond expression,
  O sweet response to voice of love divine;
Faith's joyous Yes to the assuring whisper,
  Fear not, I have redeemed thee, thou art Mine.

I am the Lord's! it hushes every murmur,
  It soothes the fevered spirit to its rest;
I am the Lord's! it is the child's rejoinder,
  Who knows and feels the Father's will is best.

I am the Lord's! yet teach me all it meaneth,
  All it involves of love and loyalty,
Of holy service, full and glad surrender,
  And unreserved obedience unto Thee.

I am the Lord's! yes; body, soul and spirit;
  They're sealed, and irrecoverably Thine;
As Thou, Belovèd, in Thy grace and fulness
  For ever and for evermore art mine.

LUCY ANN BENNETT

WILLIAM HENRY BENNETT

Bennett, William Henry (Asford, Kent, England 1843—Bath, England 1920).

W.H. Bennett was associated with assemblies of Christians, who gather in the Name of the Lord Jesus Christ. He was saved in early life and left the Church of England because of their teaching concerning Baptismal Regeneration.

The ministry of the Word given by H.W. Soltau and J.L. Harris influenced his Christian life. He spent 50 years in Yeovil assembly. His judgment on spiritual matters was valued by many believers. For many years he was the joint-editor of the magazine "Echoes of Service".

W.H. Bennett was an able writer and minister of the Word of God. He always rejoiced to exalt the Person of the Lord Jesus in all his service. The one beautiful hymn which he wrote holds a treasured place in the hearts of believers.

O CHRIST, THOU SON OF GOD

Hymn 423   Tune: *Iche Halte Treulich Still*
...*Johann Bach*

O Christ, Thou Son of God!
Thou glorious Lord of all,
Thou living One who once wast slain
Before Thy face we fall:
To Thee, O Lord, we look,
To Thee ourselves we yield;
Be Thou throughout our earthly course
Our refuge and our shield.

Lord Jesus, take our hearts,
From self-love set them free;
Help us, however dark our path,
To stay our souls on Thee:
Though evil waxes worse,
And many hearts grow cold,
Help us to cleave unto Thy name,
Thy faithful word to hold.

Help us to look beyond
The dark and gloomy night,
To wait for that blest hour when Thou
Wilt come in glory bright:
When we Thy voice shall hear,
Thy glorious face shall see,
And, like Thee, in Thy presence stand,
And ever worship Thee.

WILLIAM HENRY BENNETT

BERNARD OF CLAIRVAUX

Bernard of Clairvaux (Fontaines, France 1091—Clairvaux, France 1153).

Bernard was one of the greatest preachers and hymn writers of the Middle Ages.

His father was a knight named Jecelin, and his mother Aletta, daughter of the noble family of Mon-Bar. Jecelin perished in the Crusades, and his mother died while Bernard was a child. Following his graduation as a physician he resolved to be a monk. He founded a monastery in one of the most evil areas in France.

On account of his God-fearing life of testimony and thanksgiving, the locality became known as Clairvaux or "Bright Valley".

An interesting record is given of Bernard in Encyclopedia Britannica:

"Bernard was saturated in the language and spirit of the Scriptures... and it saved him from the grosser aberration of Medieval Catholicism."

In his sermons he seldom mentioned the "saints" or the "lady". They were overshadowed in his mind by the surpassing splendour of the Lord Jesus. The preciousness of Christ is the theme of his two greatest hymns. Both are included in the Believers Hymn Book.

LORD JESUS CHRIST, THE THOUGHT OF THEE

Hymn 137   Tune: *St. Agnes* C.M.

Lord Jesus Christ, the thought of Thee
  With sweetness fills my breast;
But sweeter far Thy face to see,
  And in Thy presence rest.

Nor voice can sing, nor heart can frame,
  Nor can the mem'ry find
A sweeter sound than Thy blest Name,
  O Saviour of mankind.

O hope of every contrite heart,
  O joy of all the meek,
To those who fall, how kind Thou art;
  How good to those who seek.

But what to those who find? Ah, this
  Nor tongue, nor pen can show;
The love of Jesus! what it is
  None but His loved ones know.

Saviour, our only joy be Thou,
  As Thou our crown wilt be;
Be Thou, O Lord, our glory now,
  And through eternity.

Jesus, Thou joy of loving hearts...................... 404

BERNARD OF CLAIRVAUX

CHRISTIAN ANDREAS BERNSTEIN

Bernstein, Christian Andreas (Domnitz, Germany, July 12, 1672—Domnitz, Oct. 18, 1699).
Bernstein's father was a Moravian pastor. He was brought to know Christ as Saviour in childhood. After finishing his studies at Halle University he was appointed a tutor in the Padagogium there. Later he was ordained as an assistant to his father, but three months later he went to be with Christ, at the age of twenty seven.

The spiritual tone of his hymns shows his deep devotion to the Lord Jesus, and his communion in the Holy Spirit.

Six of his hymns translated into English were included in the Moravian Hymn Book published in 1754.

The one selected for inclusion in the Believers Hymn Book is an example of the fervent love to the Lord of this young German.

O PATIENT, SPOTLESS ONE

Hymn 215 Tune: *Selma* S.M.

O patient, spotless One!
Our hearts in meekness train
To bear Thy yoke and learn of Thee,
That we may rest obtain.

Saviour! Thou art enough
The mind and heart to fill;
Thy life, to calm the anxious soul,
Thy love, its fear dispel.

O fix our earnest gaze
So wholly, Lord, on Thee,
That with Thy beauty occupied
We elsewhere none may see.

CHRISTIAN ANDREAS BERNSTEIN

JOHN BERRIDGE

Berridge, John (Kingston, Nottinghamshire, England. March 1, 1716—Everton, England, Jan. 22, 1793).

John Berridge was the son of a wealthy land-owner and farmer. He was educated at Clare Hall, Cambridge. After becoming a Christian through the witness of a local tailor, who was employed by his father, he dedicated his life to the preaching of the gospel, travelling many miles on horseback through the villages of Nottinghamshire. Berridge later associated with Wesley and Whitefield in the revival times which swept across the British Isles.

John Berridge wrote 342 hymns published in 1785 under the title: *"Hymns for the use of them that love and follow the Lord Jesus."*

The marriage hymn is the best known of all his hymns.

It is of interest to note that while he wrote this hymn, he never married.

LORD JESUS, WHO DIDST ONCE APPEAR

Hymn 146   Tune: *St. Bernard* C.M.

Lord Jesus, who didst once appear
　To grace a marriage feast,
We now beseech Thy presence here
　To make this wedding blest.

With grace the bride and bridegroom speed;
　Thy love their pattern be;
May heart with heart be true indeed,
　As knit, O Lord, in Thee.

With gifts of grace their hearts endow,
　Of all rich dowries best;
Their substance bless, and peace bestow,
　To sweeten all the rest.

And looking to their heavenly home,
　O may they dwell each day
As heirs of life till Thou shalt come
　To take Thy bride away.

JOHN BERRIDGE

EMMA FRANCES BEVAN

Bevan, Emma Frances (Oxford, England, Sept. 25, 1827—Cockfosters, Herts, England, Feb. 13, 1909).

Emma Frances Bevan was the daughter of an Anglican minister, Philip Shuttleworth, who became the Bishop of Chichester.

When she was twenty seven years old she was led to receive Christ as her Redeemer and Lord. Some local brethren conducted Bible Readings in the home of R. Bevan, which she attended. Later she married Bevan, who was a well known London banker. The Bevans gathered with believers in a simple assembly according to Matthew 18:20. After the death of her husband Emma Bevan spent her closing years in Cannes, France. She translated many hymns from German to English. Her contribution to hymnody was a number of Gospel hymns. The best known being:

"Sinners Jesus will receive", and "O Christ in Thee my soul hath found".

O CHRIST IN THEE MY SOUL HATH FOUND

Hymn 178   Tune: *None but Christ*

O Christ! in Thee my soul hath found,
  And found in Thee alone,
The peace, the joy I sought so long,
  The bliss till now unknown.

I sighed for rest and happiness,
  I yearned for them, not Thee;
But while I passed my Saviour by
  His love laid hold on me.

The pleasures lost I sadly mourned,
  But never wept for Thee,
Till grace the sightless eyes received
  Thy loveliness to see.

Chorus:
Now none but Christ can satisfy,
  None other Name for me;
There's love, and life, and lasting joy,
  Lord Jesus, found in Thee.

EMMA FRANCES BEVAN

EDWARD BICKERSTETH

Bickersteth, Edward (Kirkby, England, March 19, 1786—Watton, Herts, England, Feb. 28, 1850).

Edward Bickersteth was the son of a well known surgeon of Kirkby Londsdale, Westmoreland. Following his student days for the legal profession, he heard the call of God to carry the Gospel to Africa. He spent many years in West Africa among the heathen, and saw many brought to the Saviour. On returning to England he was appointed as the Secretary of the Church of England Missions.

Bickersteth was an excellent hymn writer. These were published in 1833 entitled *Christian Psalmody*. Seven of his hymns are still widely used. His hymn extolling the value of the Word of God is constantly used where believers gather to study the Holy Scriptures.

LIGHT OF THE WORLD SHINE ON OUR SOULS

Hymn 343   Tune: *Abergele* C.M.

Light of the world, shine on our souls;
   Thy grace to us afford;
And while we meet to learn Thy truth
   Be Thou our teacher, Lord.

May we its riches, power, and depth,
   Its holiness discern;
Its joyful news of saving grace
   By blest experience learn.

Thus may Thy word be dearer still,
   And studied more each day;
And as it richly dwells within,
   Thyself in it display.

EDWARD BICKERSTETH

EDWARD HENRY BICKERSTETH

Bickersteth, Edward Henry (Islington, England, Jan. 25, 1825—London, England. May 16, 1906).

Edward Henry Bickersteth was the son of Edward Bickersteth the author of the hymn "Light of the World". He was educated at Trinity College, Cambridge, and graduated with honours. Bickersteth later became the Bishop of Exeter.

He was a voluminous writer of sacred song. His writings show his faith in Christ alone for salvation, and the importance he placed upon the Holy Scriptures. Dr. Bickersteth is famous for his greatest hymn:

"Peace perfect peace, in this dark world of sin,
The blood of Jesus whispers peace within."

Another well known hymn which is often used in assemblies of believers when gathered for worship is titled "Till He come".

TILL HE COME

Hymn 299   Tune: *Wells* 7.7.7.7.7.7.

"Till He come!" O let the words
Linger on the trembling chords;
Let the "little while" between
In their golden light be seen;
Let us think how heaven and home
Lie beyond that "Till He come!"

When the weary ones we love
Enter on their rest above,
When their words of love and cheer
Fall no longer on our ear,
Hush! be every murmur dumb,
It is only "Till He come!"

Clouds and darkness round us press;
Would we have one sorrow less?
All the sharpness of the cross,
All that tells the world is loss,
Death, and darkness, and the tomb,
Pain us only "Till He come!"

Sweet the feast of love divine,
Broken bread and outpoured wine;
Sweet memorials, till the Lord
Call us round His heavenly board,
Some from earth, from glory some,
Severed only "Till He come!"

EDWARD HENRY BICKERSTETH

THOMAS BINNEY

Binney, Thomas (Newcastle-on-Tyne, England 1798—London, England, Feb. 23, 1874).

Thomas Binney was born into a poor family. He served his apprenticeship to a bookseller working from twelve to sixteen hours a day. Through reading the Bible he was led to trust Christ as his Saviour. As a student he showed no special promise, but it was soon evident that God had bestowed upon him the gift of being an evangelist. This was witnessed by the crowds that listened to him in the open air services he conducted. In 1829 he was invited to preach in an Independent church in London. Soon he was in the first rank of Metropolitan preachers. His imposing presence and impressive oratory drew large congregations to hear him. He was sound in the great doctrines of the Word of God and constantly waged war against the abuses of the State Church.

Binney wrote a valuable book on the life and ministry of Paul, also fifty books on other scriptural subjects.

He wrote two hymns, one of which is sung in assemblies of Christians.

ETERNAL LIGHT! ETERNAL LIGHT!

Hymn 378 Tune: *Newcastle* 8.6.8.8.6.

Eternal Light! eternal Light!
  How pure the soul must be
When, placed within Thy searching sight,
It shrinks not, but with calm delight
  Can live, and look on Thee.

The spirits that surround Thy throne
  May bear the burning bliss;
But that is surely theirs alone,
Since they have never, never known
  A fallen world like this.

O how shall I, whose native sphere
  Is dark, whose mind is dim,
Before the Ineffable appear,
And on my naked spirit bear
  The uncreated beam?

There is a way for man to rise
  To that sublime abode;
An offering and a sacrifice,
A Holy Spirit's energies,
  An Advocate with God.

THOMAS BINNEY

WILLIAM BLANE

Blane William (Galston, Scotland, 1859—London, England, March 11, 1936).

William Blane was saved in childhood and identified with assemblies gathered in the Name of the Lord Jesus for many years. He went to South Africa and joined J. Winsley to preach the gospel to the prospectors in the gold rush of 1884.

Blane was the author of a very valuable book of poems entitled: *Lays of Life and Hope*. Included in this volume are two outstanding poems: "The Atonement" and "Thirty Pieces of Silver", also the hymn "Kept, safely kept".

William Blane spent the last twenty years of his life in retirement in London, England.

KEPT, SAFELY KEPT

Hymn 121   Tune: *Patience* 4.6.8.8.4.

Kept, safely kept;
My fears away are swept;
In weakness to my God I cling,
Though foes be strong I calmly sing,
Kept, safely kept.

Kept by His power,
Whatever dangers lower,
The strength of God's almighty arm
Doth shield my soul from every harm,
Kept by His power.

Through simple faith,
Believing what He saith,
Unshaken on my God I lean,
And realise His power unseen,
But known to faith.

Kept all the way,
E'en to salvation's day,
His mighty love ne'er cold shall wax,
Nor shall His pow'rful grasp relax,
Through all the way.

WILLIAM BLANE

PHILIP P. BLISS

Bliss, Philipp: P.P. Bliss (Clearfield, Penn, U.S.A. July 9, 1838—Ashtabula, Ohio, U.S.A. Dec. 30, 1876).

Bliss early in his life separated the final "p" from his christian name, and made his signature P.P. Bliss.

He was saved by grace in childhood. In 1864 he was employed in Chicago by Dr. George Root, the well known musician, where he was engaged in composing Sunday School music. It soon became evident to Dr. Root that Bliss was a gifted musician and singer. He also was a man of very pleasing personality, and Christ-like in his ways. God had gifted him with a remarkable ability for writing gospel hymns and also suitable tunes for each hymn. In 1874 he joined Major Whittle, in his Gospel preaching tours, becoming his song leader, and composing new hymns for each place visited. Although a poor man Bliss gave all the Royalties on his hymns, which amounted to $30,000, a large sum in those days, to the spread of the gospel.

P.P. Bliss had a tragic death. The train in which he was travelling plunged into a river when the railway bridge gave way. He himself escaped, but in an endeavour to save his wife from a blazing car, he perished at the age of thirty eight.

The writer met the last surviving member of the Bliss family—his grand-daughter—in Australia.

Bliss wrote 48 hymns. Many of them are in popular use still. His best known gospel hymns are: "Whosoever heareth", "Almost persuaded", "I will sing of my Redeemer", "Sing them over again to me", and "Free from the law".

His most famous spiritual contribution is the beautiful song: "Man of Sorrows".

MAN OF SORROWS

Hymn 147   Tune: *Man of Sorrows* by P.P. Bliss.

"Man of Sorrows!" what a name
For the Son of God, who came
Ruined sinners to reclaim!
  Hallelujah! what a Saviour!

Bearing shame and scoffing rude
In my place condemned He stood;
Sealed my pardon with His blood:
  Hallelujah! what a Saviour!

Guilty, vile, and helpless, we;
Spotless Lamb of God was He:
"Full atonement," can it be?
  Hallelujah! what a Saviour!

"Lifted up" was He to die,
"It is finished," was His cry;
Now in heaven exalted high:
  Hallelujah! what a Saviour!

When He comes, our glorious King,
All His ransomed home to bring,
Then anew this song we'll sing:
  Hallelujah! what a Saviour!

I will sing of my Redeemer 102

PHILIP P. BLISS

JOHN ERNEST BODE

Bode, John Ernest (London, England, 1816—Castle Camps, England, 1874).

Bode was educated at Eton College and Oxford University, where he was honoured by winning the first Hertford Scholarship.

He was the Bampton Lecturer in 1855. Bode was the minister of a church in Castle Camps, Cambridgeshire for a long number of years, where he preached the Word faithfully.

He published a book of hymns in 1860 entitled: *Hymns of the Gospel*.

His well known hymn: "O Jesus I have promised to serve Thee to the end" was selected for the Believers Hymn Book Supplement in 1959.

O JESUS, I HAVE PROMISED

Hymn 425　　　Tune: *Day of Rest* 7.6.7.6.D.

O Jesus, I have promised
　To serve Thee to the end,
Be Thou for ever near me,
　My Master and my Friend;
I shall not fear the battle
　If Thou art by my side,
Nor wander from the pathway
　If Thou wilt be my guide.

O let me feel Thee near me;
　The world is ever near;
I see the sights that dazzle,
　The tempting sounds I hear;
My foes are ever near me,
　Around me and within;
But, Jesus, draw Thou nearer,
　And shield my soul from sin.

O let me see Thy footmarks,
　And in them plant mine own;
My hope to follow duly
　Is in Thy strength alone;
O guide me, call me, draw me,
　Uphold me to the end;
And then in heaven receive me,
　My Saviour and my Friend.

JOHN ERNEST BODE

JAMES BODEN

Boden, James (Chester, England. April 13, 1757— Chesterfield, England. June 4, 1841).

James Boden was born in the house formerly occupied by the well known Bible commentator; Matthew Henry, in the city of Chester, England.

At the age of sixteen he was brought by Divine grace to Christ for salvation. Keenly interested in Sunday School he built up large classes of children, and arranged well ordered instruction in the Scriptures. May of these young people were saved through his efforts. For over forty years he travelled through the Midlands of England preaching the Gospel.

Boden wrote several hymns, but very few are in use today.

One precious and inspiring hymn is still in popular use, and is included in the Believers Hymn Book.

COME ALL YE SAINTS OF GOD

Hymn 34   Tune: *Olivet* 6.6.4.6.6.6.4.

Come, all ye saints of God!
Publish through earth abroad
    Jesus' great fame:
Tell what His love has done;
Trust in His name alone;
Shout to His lofty throne,
    Worthy the Lamb!

Hence! gloomy doubts and fears;
Dry up your mournful tears;
    Swell the glad throng:
To Christ, the heavenly King,
Strike each melodious string,
From heart and voice to sing,
    Worthy's the Lamb!

Hark, how the choirs above,
Filled with the Saviour's love,
    Dwell on His name!
There, too, shall we be found,
With light and glory crowned,
While all the heavens resound
    Worthy's the Lamb!

JAMES BODEN

HORATIUS BONAR

Bonar, Horatius (Edinburgh, Scotland, Dec. 19, 1808—Edinburgh, July 31, 1889).

Bonar ranks with Watts and Wesley in the number of his living hymns, and in their present popularity. He was educated at Edinburgh University, and came to know the Lord Jesus as his personal Saviour while a student. His deliverance from the pleasures of sin is fully expressed in his best known Gospel hymn:

"I heard the voice of Jesus say,
Come unto Me and rest."

In 1837 he joined the Free Church of Scotland. He was a faithful preacher of the Gospel and was used in bringing many to Christ. Being very interested in the truth of the Lord's Second Advent, he edited "The Journal of Prophecy". In 1883 he became the Moderator of the Free Church of Scotland.

One hundred hymns which he wrote are still sung throughout the world.

His hymns were published in four hymnals which he edited: *Songs of the Wilderness* (1843); *The Bible Hymn Book* (1845); *Hymns of Faith and Hope* (1857) and *Communion Hymns* (1881).

Dr Bonar was the most eminent of all Scottish hymn writers. His hymns of communion and worship are loved and sung in hundreds of "breaking of bread" meetings, every Lord's Day.

I HEARD THE VOICE OF JESUS SAY

Hymn 90　　　Tune: *Kingsfold* D.C.M.

I heard the voice of Jesus say,
　"Come unto Me and rest;
Lay down, thou weary one, lay down
　Thy head upon My breast."

I came to Jesus as I was,
　Weary, and worn, and sad;
I found in Him a resting-place,
　And He has made me glad.

All that I was—my sin, my guilt........................ 8
Blessed be God, our God.............................. 24
Christ hath done the mighty work 33
Done is the work that saves........................... 45
For the bread and for the wine........................ 49
I bless the Christ of God 86
I hear the words of love 91
I was a wandering sheep 105
My sins were laid on Jesus........................... 166
No blood, no altar now 171
Praise, praise ye the Name of Jehovah 228
Sun and Shield, O Lord, art Thou 255
Here, O our Lord, we see Thee face to face 339
Go labour on; spend, and be spent 387

HORATIUS BONAR

ROBERT BOSWELL

Boswell, Robert (Ayrshire, Scotland, 1764—London, England, 1804).
Robert Boswell was an excellent Hebrew scholar. After his conversion he joined the followers of John Glas, a leading dissenting minister from the Church of Scotland, and was chosen to be the leading elder in the Glasite congregation at Edinburgh.

He published a Revised Version of the Scottish version of the Psalms in 1784.

His best known contribution to hymnody is included in the Believers Hymn Book.

Boswell died suddenly in the pulpit while preaching the Gospel in London.

BEHOLD, WHAT LOVE, WHAT BOUNDLESS LOVE

Hymn 26   Tune: *Boundless*

Behold, what love, what boundless love,
   The Father hath bestowed
On sinners lost, that we should be
   Now called the sons of God.

No longer far from Him, but now
   By precious blood made nigh;
Accepted in the Well-beloved,
   Near to God's heart we lie.

What we in glory soon shall be,
   It doth not yet appear;
But when our precious Lord we see,
   We shall His image bear.

With such a blessed hope in view,
   We would more holy be,
More like our risen, glorious Lord,
   Whose face we soon shall see.

Chorus:
"Behold... what manner of love... what manner of love the Father hath bestowed upon us, that we... that we should be called... should be called the sons of God."

ROBERT BOSWELL

FRANCIS BOTTOME

Bottome, Francis (Derby, England, May 26, 1823— Tavistock, Devon, England, 1894).

Francis Bottome was converted when very young. He moved to the U.S.A. in 1850 and entered the ministry of the Methodist Church. He was a gifted speaker and musician. He assisted in the compilation of *Smith's Gospel Hymn Book* in 1872.

Bottome was the author of six choice hymns.

His well known "O joy of the justified, joy of the free" is sung by Christians in every place where the Name of the Lord Jesus is honoured.

O JOY OF THE JUSTIFIED, JOY OF THE FREE

Hymn 186   Tune: *Mighty Love*

O joy of the justified, joy of the free!
I'm washed in that crimson tide opened
    for me;
In Christ, my Redeemer, rejoicing I stand,
And point to the print of the nail in His hand.

    O sing of His mighty love,
      Sing of His mighty love,
    Sing of His mighty love,
      Mighty to save!

Lord Jesus, the crucified, now Thou art mine;
Though once a lost sinner, yet now I am
    Thine;
In conscious salvation I sing of His grace,
Who lifts now upon me the smile of His
    face.

Lord Jesus, my Saviour, I'll still sing of Thee,
Yes, sing of Thy precious blood poured out for
    me;
And when in the mansions of glory above,
I'll praise and adore Thine unchangeable love.

FRANCIS BOTTOME

MATTHEW BRIDGES

Bridges, Matthew (Maldon, Essex, England. July 14, 1800—Sidmouth, Devon, England. Oct. 6, 1894).

The dominant interests of Matthew Bridges were literature and history. He wrote a very interesting history: *The Roman Empire under Constantine the Great*. His famous poem "Jerusalem Regained" was published in 1825. Later in 1852 he authored the well known hymn "Crown Him with many crowns". The many crowns were suggested by Revelation 19:12.

Matthew was the brother of Charles Bridges, who was an able Bible Expositor. His exposition of the book of Proverbs is a classic work. In his later years Matthew Bridges was brought under the influence of the Oxford Movement and followed John Henry Newman into the Roman Catholic Church. His last days were spent in Quebec, Canada.

CROWN HIM WITH MANY CROWNS

Hymn 376   Tune: *Diademata* D.S.M.

Crown Him with many crowns,
The Lamb upon His throne;
Hark! how the heavenly anthem drowns
All music but its own;
Awake, my soul, and sing
Of Him who died for thee,
And hail Him as thy matchless King
Through all eternity.

Crown Him the Lord of love;
Behold His hands and side;
Rich wounds, yet visible above
In beauty glorified;
All hail, Redeemer hail!
For Thou hast died for me:
Thy praise shall never, never fail
Throughout eternity.

MATTHEW BRIDGES

GEORGE BURDEN BUBIER

Bubier, George Burden (Reading, England, Feb. 2, 1823—Acocks Green, England, March 19, 1869).

George Bubier was the son of an Independent minister in Reading.

He trusted Christ as his Saviour early in life. After working in the Bank of England at Banbury, he resigned to prepare himself for the ministry at Homerton Congregational College. He was known as a fearless preacher of the Word of God.

Bubier wrote many hymns which were included in a hymnal published in 1855: *Hymns and Sacred Songs*.

The most popular of this author's hymns is titled "Longing after God". It appears in many hymn books. The second verse has been admired by many poets and hymn writers.

I WOULD COMMUNE WITH THEE, MY GOD

Hymn 100 Tune: *St. Anne* C.M.

I would commune with Thee, my God;
  E'en to Thy seat I come;
I leave my joys, I leave my sins,
  And seek in Thee my home.

I stand upon the mount of God,
  With sunlight in my soul;
I hear the storms in vales beneath;
  I hear the thunders roll.

But I am calm with Thee, my God,
  Beneath these glorious skies;
And to the height on which I stand
  Nor storms nor clouds can rise.

O this is life! O this is joy!
  My God, to find Thee so;
Thy face to see, Thy voice to hear,
  And all Thy love to know.

GEORGE BURDEN BUBIER

GEORGE BURDER

Burder, George (London, England, June 5, 1752—London, England, May 29, 1832).

George Burder was saved listening to the preaching of George Whitefield. He was a gifted artist, but at the age of twenty three decided to spend his time and talent preaching the Gospel.

He was the founder of the British and Foreign Bible Society. He also published a series of much used Gospel tracts for sailors called "Sea Sermons", which led to many conversions.

Burder also authored many hymns and collected the hymns of others in a well known hymnal called *Collected Hymns by Various Writers* in 1784. One of his own hymns has been widely sung in assemblies throughout the world, and is included in the Believers Hymn Book.

George Burder continued to preach until shortly before his homecall in his eightieth year. He was a faithful servant of Christ.

GOD IS LOVE

Hymn 41   Tune: *Colchester* C.M.

Come, ye that know the Saviour's name,
  And raise your thoughts above;
Let every heart and voice unite
  To sing—that God is love!

His Word this precious truth reveals,
  And all His mercies prove;
Creation and redemption join
  To show—that God is love!

His work begun is carried on
  By power from heaven above;
And every step, from first to last,
  Declares—that God is love!

O may we all, while here below,
  His perfect will approve,
Till nobler songs, in brighter worlds,
  Proclaim—that God is love!

GEORGE BURDER

HANNAH KILHAM BURLINGHAM

Burlingham, Hannah Kilham (Evesham, England, March 17, 1842—Evesham, England, May 15, 1901).

Hannah Burlingham was brought up in the atmosphere of a Christian home. At twelve years of age she became a believer.

Her desire to obey the Lord led her later to associate with a company of Christians, who were gathered to the Lord's Name alone. It was said of her as a young Christian that she loved the Lord, the Scriptures and the Lord's people fervently. Her poetic ability coupled with spiritual depth is expressed in the many hymns which she authored.

She also translated many hymns from German, including "Lord Jesus, Friend unfailing" (Hymn 131) which was written by Samuel Christian Gottlieb Kuster, who died in 1865.

Six of her hymns are in the Believers Hymn Book. The best known among brethren being "I'm waiting for Thee, Lord, Thy beauty to see, Lord". This revealed her joyous anticipation of the Lord's return.

JESUS CHRIST, THOU KING OF GLORY

Hymn 110   Tune: *Star of Peace*

Jesus Christ, Thou King of Glory,
  Born a Saviour-Prince to be,
While the angel-hosts adore Thee,
        We joy in Thee,
Singing of Thy grace the story,
        Praise, praise to Thee.

Thou the ransom price hast given,
  Setting thus the captive free;
Thou art Lord of earth and heaven;
        We joy in Thee.
Through Thy blood we stand forgiven,
        Praise, praise to Thee.

Bright, bright home! Beyond the Skies 22
Heirs of salvation, chosen of God! 69
I'm waiting for Thee, Lord,
  Thy beauty to see, Lord 84
O God of matchless grace,
  we sing unto Thy Name! 185
The glory shines before me 263

HANNAH KILHAM BURLINGHAM

WILLIAM CAMERON

Cameron, William (Ballater, Scotland, 1751—Kirknewton, 1811).
William Cameron was the son of a farmer. He studied at the Marischal College, Aberdeen, for the ministry of the Church of Scotland. He became friendly with Dr. Beattie, author of *The Minstrel.*

Dr. Beattie recognised the poetic talent of Cameron, and commended him to the Committee of the Church of Scotland, which was then revising the Paraphrases. He was given chief responsibilities in this work of revision. Two Paraphrases were added by him, and he revised thirty three others. He also published a valuable book: *Poems on Various Subjects.* William Cameron wrote a number of excellent hymns, two of these are included in the Believers Hymn Book.

BLEST BE THE EVERLASTING GOD

Hymn 369　　　Tune: *Bishopthorpe*

Blest be the everlasting God,
　The Father of our Lord;
Be His abounding mercy praised,
　His majesty adored.

When from the dead He raised His Son,
　And called Him to the sky,
He gave our souls a lively hope
　That they should never die.

Saints by the power of God are kept
　Till the salvation come;
We walk by faith as strangers here,
　But Christ shall call us home.

Blest morning, whose first dawning rays 370

WILLIAM CAMERON

MARGARET LEDLEY CARSON

Carson, Margaret Ledley (Coleraine, Nth. Ireland, 1833—Portrush, Nth. Ireland, Feb. 24, 1920).

Margaret Ledley Carson was the daughter of Dr. G. Carson, a medical practitioner in Coleraine. Early in life she came to know Christ as her Saviour and Lord and later wrote a number of hymns and poems. Her best known composition being: "My chains are snapt, the bonds of sin are broken". Soon after writing four verses of this hymn in her notebook she showed them to C.H. Mackintosh. When he read the words he appreciated them as they presented the Person of Christ, but commented that it did not include the theme of the Lord's return, and taking his pencil added the delightful fifth verse: "We wait to see the Morning Star appearing".

It is interesting to note that Margaret Carson financed the building of the Gospel Hall in Portrush.

MY CHAINS ARE SNAPT

Hymn 152   Tune: *Palm* 11.4.11.4.

My chains are snapt, the bonds of sin are broken,
    And I am free;
O let the triumphs of His grace be spoken,
    Who died for me.

O death! O grave! I do not dread your power,
    The ransom's paid;
On Jesus, in that dark and dreadful hour,
    My guilt was laid.

Yes, Jesus bore it, bore, in love unbounded,
    What none can know;
He passed through death, and gloriously confounded
    Our every foe.

And now He's risen, proclaim the joyful story,
    The Lord's on high;
And we in Him are raised to endless glory,
    And ne'er can die.

verse written by C.H.M.
We wait to see the Morning Star appearing
    In glory bright;
This blessèd hope illumes, with beams most cheering,
    The hours of night.

MARGARET LEDLEY CARSON

MARY CARTER

Carter, Mary (c. 1875).
Mary Carter was the daughter of Dr. Carter, one of the brethren associated with J.N. Darby, J.G. Bellett, A.N. Groves, Lady Powerscourt, and others of the early brethren. She attended the Bible Readings where the great truths pertaining to assembly gathering and the Lord's return were studied. She became a devoted believer and wrote many spiritual hymns. Many of these are in *Hymns of Light and Love* and two are included in the *Believers Hymn Book*.

The beautiful words of "On Thy broken body feeding" is often sung when saints are assembled to proclaim the Lord's Death in the "breaking of bread."

ON THY BROKEN BODY FEEDING

Hymn 214   Tune: *Russian Melody*

On Thy broken body feeding,
   Lord, our hearts in one unite;
Here our souls behold Thee bleeding,
   Put to grief in sinners' sight.
O that Jesus thus should love us,
   Love us unto death and shame!
Let the dear remembrance move us,
   While we meet in His blest Name.

Here the pledge of Thy returning
   Tells of all the joys of home,
And our hearts within us burning,
   Cry "Amen, Lord Jesus, come!"
Soon, full soon, we thus together
   In the Father's house shall meet;
And the heavenly courts for ever
   Tread with undefilèd feet.

Through the dark path of sorrow 293

MARY CARTER

JOHN CENNICK

Cennick, John (Reading, England, Dec. 12, 1718—London, July 4, 1755).

Born of Quaker parents, John Cennick had a very strict religious background, however, on moving to London to study his profession as a land surveyor, he became a wild and reckless young man. He was taken up with gambling and drunkenness. When twenty one years old God gave him concern of soul and he was saved listening to the faithful preaching of George Whitefield. He began to preach the gospel to the colliers at Kingswood, and became associated with the Wesleys as a lay preacher. Because of differences in doctrine he later parted from the Wesleys and became a Moravian Brethren preacher, spending most of his later years in Gracehill, Northern Ireland. He died at the early age of thirty seven after serving the Lord faithfully for sixteen years. His greatest hymn is still a favourite in assemblies of the Lord's people:
>"Brethren, let us join to bless
>Jesus Christ, our joy and peace."

JESUS CHRIST OUR JOY AND PEACE

Hymn 20   Tune: *The Cross* 7.7.7.7.

Brethren, let us join to bless
Jesus Christ our joy and peace;
Him, who bowed His head so low
Underneath our load of woe.

His the curse, the wounds, the gall,
His the stripes—He bore them all;
His the dying cry of pain
When our sins He did sustain.

Praise our God who willed it thus;
Praise the Lamb who died for us;
Praise the Father, through the Son,
Who so vast a work hath done.

Lo, He comes! with clouds descending. 408

This hymn was compositely composed with Charles Wesley, Martin Madan, and John Cennick.

JOHN CENNICK

HENRY D'ARCY CHAMPNEY

Champney, Henry D'Arcy (Tunbridgewells, England, 1854— London, England, 1942).

One of the greatest hymns sung in Christian worship was composed by Henry D'Arcy Champney. This is: "Jesus, our Lord, with what joy we adore Thee." This is the only hymn on record from his pen, but it is a legacy to the Church. The language is a beautiful epitomy of the Person and Work of our Lord Jesus Christ, the Worthy One.

Champney was associated with such brethren as C.A. Coates and C.H. Macintosh. He went to be with Christ in his eighty ninth year.

JESUS, OUR LORD, WITH WHAT JOY WE ADORE THEE

Hymn 402   10.10.11.10

Jesus, our Lord, with what joy we adore
  Thee,
 Chanting our praise to Thyself on the
  throne,
Blest in Thy presence, we worship before
  Thee,
 Own Thou art worthy, and worthy alone.

Verily God, yet become truly human—
 Lower than angels—to die in our stead;
How hast Thou, long promised Seed of the
  woman,
 Trod on the serpent and bruisèd his head!

How didst Thou humble Thyself to be taken,
 Led by Thy creatures, and nailed to the
  cross?
Hated of men, and of God, too, forsaken,
 Shunning not darkness, the curse, and the
  loss.

How hast Thou triumphed, and triumphed
  with glory,
 Battled death's forces, rolled back every
  wave!
Can we refrain, then, from telling the story,
 How Thou art victor o'er death and
  the grave?

HENRY D'ARCY CHAMPNEY

ROBERT CLEAVER CHAPMAN

Chapman, Robert Cleaver (Denmark, Jan. 4, 1803— Barnstaple, England, Jan. 12, 1902).

Robert Cleaver Chapman had the inestimable privilege of a godly mother who stored his mind with the Scriptures. He was sent from Denmark to England to complete his education and graduated as a lawyer.

The turning point came in his life when he heard James Harrington Evans preach the Gospel. Through this devoted servant of Christ he trusted Christ as his Saviour and Lord. He was baptised and came into fellowship with an assembly of Christians in London. Later, when called by God to minister the gospel, he was told by the brethren that he would never make a preacher. His reply was: "There are many who preach Christ, but my aim will be to live Christ." This is what he did for eighty years. R.C. Chapman wrote 165 hymns published in a rare volume *Hymns and Meditations.* Eight of these are in the Believers Hymn Book and are sung in Christian assemblies, especially when gathered to remember the Lord.

R.C. Chapman was never married. He departed to be with his Lord in his one hundredth year, having served Him for eighty years.

WITH JESUS IN OUR MIDST

Hymn 325   Tune: *Selma. Isle of Arran Melody*

With Jesus in our midst,
We gather round the board;
Though many, we are one in Christ,
One body in the Lord.

Our sins were laid on Him
When bruised on Calvary;
With Christ we died and rose again,
And sit with Him on high.

Faith eats the bread of life,
And drinks the living wine;
Thus we, in love together knit,
On Jesus' breast recline.

Soon shall the night be gone,
And we with Jesus reign;
The marriage supper of the Lamb
Shall banish all our pain.

No bone of Thee was broken 167
Jesus, in His Heavenly Temple 111
No condemnation O my soul 162
My soul amid this stormy world 164
O our Saviour crucified 210
The Lamb of God to slaughter led 271
The Lord of Glory! Who is He? 276

ROBERT CLEAVER CHAPMAN

ELIZABETH RUNDLE CHARLES

Charles, Elizabeth Rundle (Tavistock, England, Jan. 2, 1828—Hampstead Heath, London, England, March 28, 1896).

Elizabeth Rundle Charles was the daughter of a Member of the British House of Commons. Her husband was Andrew Charles, a Barrister of law.

She was a talented poet and musician. As a translator of hymns she became well known. Her many writings especially in the realm of history are of great value. In 1864 she published *Voice of Christian Life in Song*. Her famous hymn on the Annunciation appeared in her book *The Three Wakings*.

"No Gospel Like this feast," her hymn which is suitable for the Lord's Supper, is included in the Believers Hymn Book.

NO GOSPEL LIKE THIS FEAST

Hymn 421   Tune: *Sandys* S.M.

No gospel like this feast
Spread for us, Lord, by Thee;
No prophets or evangelists
Preach the glad news more free.

All our redemption cost,
All our redemption won;
All it has won for us, the lost,
All it cost Thee, the Son.

Thine was the bitter price,
Ours is the free gift given;
Thine was the blood of sacrifice,
Ours is the wine of heaven.

Here we would rest midway
As on a sacred height;
That darkest and that brightest day
Meeting before our sight.

From that dark depth of woes
Thy love for us has trod,
We soar to heights of blest repose
Thy love prepares with God.

ELIZABETH RUNDLE CHARLES

TOBIAS CLAUSNITZER

Clausnitzer, Tobias (Thum, Germany, Feb. 5, 1619— Weiden, Germany, May 7, 1684).

Tobias Clausnitzer graduated from the University of Leipzig. He was a chaplain in the army for many years. In this capacity he had the honour of preaching on the occasion of the coronation of Christina, as Queen of Sweden. He also preached at the thanksgiving service at the command of General Wrangel, in Upper Palatine, on Jan. 1, 1649, after the peace treaty of Westphalia.

This devoted and faithful Christian penned seven great hymns.

LOOK UPON US BLESSED LORD

Hymn 411   Tune: *Liebster Jesu*

Look upon us, blessèd Lord,
Take our wandering thoughts and guide us;
  We have come to hear Thy word;
With Thy teaching now provide us,
That, from earth's distractions turning,
We Thy message may be learning.

Brightness of the Father's face,
Light of light, from God proceeding,
  Make us ready in this place;
Ear and heart await Thy leading:
In our study, prayers and praising,
May our souls find their upraising.

TOBIAS CLAUSNITZER

ELIZABETH CECILIA CLEPHANE

Clephane, Elizabeth Cecilia (Edinburgh, Scotland. June 18, 1830—Melrose, Scotland, Feb. 19, 1869).

Elizabeth Clephane's father was the sheriff of Fifeshire. Her parents were Christians, so she came to know Christ as her Saviour in childhood. For a number of years she resided with her brother in Fergus, Ontario, Canada. This devoted Christian wrote eight beautiful hymns, which were published posthumously in 1872 in *The Family Treasury*, a Free Church of Scotland magazine. It was from this paper that Ira. D. Sankey found the hymn "The Ninety and Nine", and composed the music. She also wrote the beautiful words of "Beneath the Cross of Jesus" four years before her home call. It is believed that these two well known hymns were written at Fergus. These hymns were not discovered until years after her death at the age of thirty nine. They are given a first line position by all hymnologists.

BENEATH THE CROSS

Hymn 23   Tune: *Refuge* P.M.

Beneath the Cross of Jesus
  I fain would take my stand,
The shadow of a mighty Rock
  Within a weary land;
A home within the wilderness,
  A rest upon the way,
From the burning of the noontide heat
  And the burden of the day.

Upon the Cross of Jesus,
  Mine eye at times can see
The very dying form of One
  Who suffered there for me;
And from my smitten heart with tears,
  Two wonders I confess,
The wonder of His glorious love,
  And my own worthlessness.

I take the Cross of Jesus
  For my abiding place;
I ask no other sunshine than
  The sunshine of His face;
Content to let the world go by,
  To know no gain nor loss:
My sinful self my only shame,
  My glory all the Cross.

ELIZABETH CECILIA CLEPHANE

ELIZABETH CODNER

Codner, Elizabeth (Dartmouth, England, 1824—Croydon, England, March 28, 1919).

Elizabeth Codner, nee Harris, was the wife of a Church of Scotland minister. She was associated with the Mildmay Mission work in North London for many years. In connection with this work among women she edited a monthly paper: *Woman and Christ*.

During the 1859 revival in Ireland she was inspired to write the well known hymn: "Lord I hear of showers of blessing." This beautiful hymn is the only recorded song written by Elizabeth Codner. Seven of the original verses are included in Hymn 139 in the *Believers Hymn Book*.

LORD TO THEE MY HEART ASCENDING

Hymn 139   Tune: *Even me*

Lord! to Thee my heart ascending
  For Thy mercy full and free,
Thankful sings for grace transcending,
  Grace vouchsafed to sinful me,
        Even me.

Holy Father! who with yearning
  Of eternal love didst see
Hatred in my bosom burning,
  Thou didst give Thy Son for me,
        Even me.

Precious Saviour! great Redeemer!
  Praise, eternal praise to Thee;
Though so long a wand'ring sinner,
  Thou hast kindly welcomed me,
        Even me.

Can it be that I, an alien,
  Now a child shall ever be?
Can it be that, all forgiven,
  Glory is prepared for me?
        Even me.

ELIZABETH CODNER

JOSIAH CONDOR

Condor, Josiah (London, England, Sept. 17, 1789—St. John's Wood, London, Dec. 27, 1855).

Josiah Condor was the son of a bookseller. His parents were God-fearing Christians. He was saved in childhood. At an early age he lost the sight of his right eye, and fearing the other might be affected he was sent by his parents to be treated by a noted eye-doctor. While undergoing treatment the doctor became tutor to the boy who gave evidence of great ability in writing poems. He became a prolific hymn writer and was the compiler of *The Congregational Hymnal* in 1836. Dr. Julian the eminent hymnologist ranks Condor as the best writer of his time, and states that his hymns are the outcome of a deeply spiritual mind.

His best known hymn "Thou art the Everlasting Word" expresses in delightful language the greatness of Christ—the Father's Only Son.

THE EVERLASTING WORD

Hymn 352   Tune: *Arabia*

Thou art the Everlasting Word,
  The Father's only Son,
God manifestly seen and heard,
  And heaven's belovèd One.

  Worthy, O Lamb of God, art Thou,
  That every knee to Thee should bow!

In Thee, most perfectly expressed,
  The Father's glories shine,
Of the full Deity possessed,
  Eternally divine!

But the high myst'ries of His name
  An angel's grasp transcend;
The Father only (glorious claim!)
  The Son can comprehend.

Throughout the universe of bliss,
  The centre Thou, and Sun,
Th' eternal theme of praise is this,
  To heaven's belovèd One.

JOSIAH CONDOR

ANN ROSS COUSIN

Cousin, Ann Ross (Beith, Scotland, April 27, 1824—Melrose, Scotland, Dec. 6, 1906).
  Ann Cousin was the only daughter of Dr. David Cundell. She became a Christian as a school girl. She married William Cousin, who was a minister of the Free Church of Scotland in Melrose.
  Following her marriage she began writing poems and hymns. These were published in a volume called *Immanuel's Land* in 1876.
  Ann Ross Cousin won her reputation as a poet by writing, *The last words of Samuel Rutherford*. The well known hymn "The sands of time are sinking" is part of this poem. After reading over two hundred letters written by Rutherford, during his two years of captivity for his faithfulness to the Truth, she wrote her poem of nineteen stanzas (152 lines). It has been called one of the great hymns of Christian faith and testimony. Her other well known hymn, "O Christ what burdens bowed Thy head" sets forth in touching language the substitutive character of the Atoning Death of the Blessed Lord. Both hymns are in the Believers Hymn Book.

O CHRIST, WHAT BURDENS BOWED THY HEAD

Hymn 176 Tune: *Substitution*

O Christ, what burdens bowed Thy head!
　Our load was laid on Thee;
Thou stoodest in the sinner's stead,
　Bear'st all my ill for me.
A victim led, Thy blood was shed;
　Now there's no load for me.

IMMANUEL'S LAND
Hymn 190 Tune: *Rutherford*

O Christ! He is the fountain,
　The deep, sweet well of love;
The streams on earth I've tasted,
　More deep I'll drink above;
There, to an ocean's fulness,
　His mercy doth expand,
And glory, glory dwelleth
　In Immanuel's land.

When we reach our peaceful dwelling 353

ANN ROSS COUSIN

WILLIAM COWPER

Cowper, William (Berkhamstead, England, Nov. 15. 1731—East Dekeham, England April 25, 1800).

William Cowper has been described as the greatest poet of his age. His father was chaplain to King George the second, and his brother became Lord Chancellor and the first Lord Cowper.

Cowper graduated as a lawyer and was called to the Bar in 1754. About this time he also heard the call of God by the Spirit, and through faith in Christ became a devoted Christian. However he suffered seasons of deep melancholy. A family named Ulwin befriended him and invited him to reside with them at Olney, where John Newton preached. He and Newton joined in evangelistic work, and in the production of what was known as *Olney Hymns*. Cowper's poem "The Task" was widely acclaimed, and he became one of England's greatest poets. His hymns are beautiful in language and of great spiritual depth. Six of his hymns are included in the Believers Hymn Book.

THERE IS A FOUNTAIN

Hymn 274　　　Tune: *Windsor*

There is a fountain filled with blood,
　Drawn from Immanuel's veins,
And sinners plunged beneath that flood
　Lose all their guilty stains.

The dying thief rejoiced to see
　That fountain in his day;
And there have I, as vile as he,
　Washed all my sins away.

Dear dying Lamb! Thy precious blood
　Shall never lose its power,
Till all the ransomed Church of God
　Be saved, to sin no more.

God moves in a mysterious way. Tune:
　St. Anne... 53
Hark! my soul, it is the Lord. Tune:
　St. Bess... 63
I thirst, but not as once I did. Tune:
　Lichfield 98
My Saviour, whom absent, I love. Tune:
　David.. 161
O Lord, where'er Thy people meet. Tune:
　Broughton 204

WILLIAM COWPER

EMILY MAY CRAWFORD

Crawford, Emily May (Lambeth, England. May 10, 1864—Folkeston, England, July 9, 1927).

Emily May Crawford (nee Grimes) became a Christian in her teen-age years. When she was twenty nine years of age she was called of God to teach children in the mission station of Pondoland, Africa. There she married Dr. Crawford, who was a missionary. The Crawfords spent their lives in the mission field at Kikuyu, British East Africa, where God blessed their work in the salvation of many souls.

Her hymn "Speak Lord in the stillness" was first published in the magazine *Gleaner.* in 1896.

SPEAK, LORD, IN THE STILLNESS

Hymn 445   Tune: *St. Wystan*

Speak, Lord, in the stillness,
   While I wait on Thee;
Hushed my heart to listen
   In expectancy.

Speak, O Blessèd Master,
   In this quiet hour;
Let me see Thy face, Lord,
   Feel Thy touch of power.

For the words Thou speakest,
   They are life indeed;
Living Bread from heaven
   Now my spirit feed.

Like a watered garden,
   Full of fragrance rare,
Lingering in Thy presence
   Let my life appear.

EMILY MAY CRAWFORD

JANE CREWDSON

Crewdson, Jane (Cornwall, England, 1809—Manchester, England, 1863).

This devoted Christian hymn writer was very frail and for the greater part of her life a confined invalid. Her husband, Tom Crewdson, was a large manufacturer in Manchester. Although so afflicted with pain and weakness her spiritual life was evident. She writes of the sufficiency of the Lord and His sympathy all the days of her life. Between periods of extreme suffering she penned many beautiful hymns. These were published under the title "A Little While" in 1864, a year after her home call. Three of her hymns are included in the Believers Hymn Book.

O THOU WHOSE BOUNTY FILLS OUR CUP

Hymn 332   Tune: *Abridge*

O Thou, whose bounty fills our cup
  With every blessing meet!
We give Thee thanks for every drop,
  The bitter and the sweet.

We thank Thee for the desert road,
  And for the river side;
For all Thy goodness has bestowed,
  And all Thy grace denied.

We thank Thee for the smile and frown,
  And for the gain and loss;
We bless Thee for the future crown,
  And for the present cross.

We bless Thee for the glad increase,
  And for the waning joy;
And for the calm and settled peace
  Which nothing can destroy.

I've found a joy in sorrow. Tune:
  Salvator 104
O for the peace that floweth as a river. Tune:
  Shemah 192

JANE CREWDSON

WILLIAM ORCUTT CUSHING

Cushing, William Orcutt (Hingham, Mass. U.S.A. Dec. 31, 1823—Lisbon, New York, Oct. 19, 1902).

William Cushing was a faithful preacher of the Gospel in New York State for over twenty years. Following the death of his wife he lost his power of speech. Overcome with deep despair he looked to the Lord to give him some future service. His prayer was answered and God gave him a wonderful ability and unusual gift in writing spiritual songs. These came to the attention of Ira D. Sankey and formed some of the theme hymns in the great gospel meetings conducted by D.L. Moody.

William Orcutt Cushing wrote over three hundred hymns, among them the well known children's hymn "When He cometh, When He cometh, to make up His jewels." He also wrote the beautiful hymn concerning his own experiences "Hiding in Thee".

HIDING IN THEE

Hymn 345   Tune: *Hiding in Thee* by Sankey

O safe to the Rock that is higher than I,
My soul in its conflicts and sorrows
  would fly;
So sinful, so weary, Thine, Thine would I be;
Thou blest Rock of Ages, I'm hiding in
  Thee.

  Hiding in Thee, hiding in Thee,
  Thou blest Rock of Ages, I'm hiding in
    Thee.

How oft in the conflict, when pressed by the
  foe,
I have fled to my Refuge, and breathed out
  my woe;
How often, when trials like sea-billows roll,
Have I hidden in Thee, O Thou Rock of my
  soul!

WILLIAM ORCUTT CUSHING

MARY S.B. DANA

Dana, Mary Stanley Bunce (Beaufort, S.C., U.S.A. Feb. 15, 1810—Texas, U.S.A. Feb. 8, 1883).

Mary Dana, *nee* Palmer, wrote the beautiful hymn "I'm a Pilgrim, and a Stranger" while living in Iowa, where her husband died. She is known in hymnology by the name Dana, though afterwards she became Mrs. Shindler.

The tune identified with this hymn is untraced, save that it is said to be an "Italian Air" and that its original title was "*Buono Notte*" (good night).

As Mary S.B. Dana she wrote a number of hymns published in two volumes: *The Northern Harp* and *The Southern Harp*.

The hymn included in the Believers Hymn Book expresses the ardent faith of the writer and the Blessed Hope of being with Christ in glory.

I'M A PILGRIM

Hymn 83   Tune: *Italian Air*

I'm a pilgrim and a stranger,
    Rough and thorny is the road,
Often in the midst of danger,
    But it leads to God.
Clouds and darkness oft distress me,
    Great and many are my foes;
Anxious cares and thoughts oppress me:
    But my Father knows.

I shall then with joy behold Him,
    Face to face my Saviour see;
Fall with rapture and adore Him
    For His love to me.
Nothing more shall then distress me
    In the land of sweet repose;
Jesus stands engaged to bless me:
    This my Father knows.

MARY S.B. DANA

JOHN NELSON DARBY

Darby, John Nelson (London, England, Nov. 18, 1800—Bournemouth, England, April 11, 1882).

John Nelson Darby was the youngest son of John Darby of Leaps Castle, Kings County, Ireland. His mother was of the Vaughan family, well known in Wales. Sir Henry Darby, his uncle, was the Commander of the "Beleerophan", and served under Lord Nelson, at the battle of the Nile in 1798. John Nelson Darby was sponsored by Lord Nelson at his baptism, and given his middle name. He graduated from Trinity College, Dublin in 1819 winning the Classical Gold Medal. Later in 1820 he entered the legal profession. At the age of twenty three he was saved through reading the Scriptures, and left his vocation, believing God had called him to serve Him. He became a clergyman of the Church of England and began his ministry in a large parish in Wicklow, Ireland. John Nelson Darby soon found that the condition and teachings of the Church of England were contrary to what the Scriptures taught. With a number of other concerned believers who gathered in the mansion of Lady Powerscourt in Ireland, Bible Readings to search the Word of God commenced. There it was found that the early Christians in Apostolic days gathered to Break Bread in remembrance of the Lord (Acts 20:7). The great truth of the imminent return of Christ for His Church became to them a glorious Hope, to be expected at any moment. John Nelson Darby resigned from the Church of England to gather alone to the Name of the Lord Jesus with fellow believers of kindred spirit. He became one of the most widely travelled of the brethren, preaching the Gospel and ministering the Word in Europe, North America and Australia.

His written ministry was extensive and valuable, and his New Translation of the Bible widely accepted as one of the most reliable. As the author of many hymns of devotion to the Person of Christ he rightfully holds an honoured place in the realm of hymnology. Five of these are included in the Believers Hymn Book, being frequently sung in assemblies of the Lord's people.

HARK! TEN THOUSAND VOICES CRYING

Hymn 65   Tune: *Laus Deo* 8.7.8.7.

Hark! ten thousand voices crying,
  "Lamb of God!" with one accord;
Thousand, thousand saints replying,
  Wake at once the echoing chord.

"Praise the Lamb," the chorus waking,
  All in heaven together throng,
Loud and far, each tongue partaking,
  Rolls along the endless song.

Grateful incense this, ascending
  Ever to the Father's throne;
Every knee to Jesus bending,
  All the mind in heaven is one.

All the Father's counsels claiming
  Equal honours to the Son;
All the Son's effulgence beaming,
  Makes the Father's glory known.

O Lord Thy love's unbounded 206
Rise, my soul, Thy God directs thee 239
This world is a wilderness wide 298
And is it so—we shall be like Thy Son 366

JOHN NELSON DARBY

ELIZABETH DARK
(MARIANNE NUNN)

Dark, Elizabeth (Colchester, England, May 17, 1778—Colchester, 1847).

Elizabeth Dark is better known as Marianne Nunn. Elizabeth Dark is a *Nom De Plume*.

She lived the greater part of her life in retirement, and was never married. In the solitude of her home in Colchester she wrote many beautiful spiritual hymns. These were published in a book called *The Christian Lyre* in 1830. Her hymn "One there is above all others" is famous and widely used. This hymn is the one by which she is best remembered.

"Inside the vail—Outside the camp" is a hymn often sung by believers when gathered to worship.

ONE THERE IS ABOVE ALL OTHERS

Hymn 213   Tune: *Tenderness*

One there is above all others;
O how He loves!
His is love beyond a brother's;
O how He loves!
Earthly friends may fail or leave us,
One day soothe, the next day grieve us,
But this Friend will ne'er deceive us;
O how He loves!

We have found a friend in Jesus;
O how He loves!
'Tis His great delight to bless us;
O how He loves!
How our hearts delight to hear Him
Bid us dwell in safety near Him!
Why should we distrust or fear Him?
O how He loves!

Through Thy Precious Body Broken. Tune: *Tenderness* 289

Both the hymns included in the Believers Hymn Book by Elizabeth Dark are sung to the same Tune "Tenderness" composed by Richard Beaty.

ELIZABETH DARK—MARIANNE NUNN

SAMUEL DAVIES

Davies, Samuel (Newcastle, Delaware, U.S.A. Nov. 3, 1724—Princeton, U.S.A. Feb. 3, 1761).

Samuel Davies had a devoted Christian mother. At the age of fifteen he trusted Christ as his Saviour and became an earnest believer, giving himself to the serious study of the Scriptures. When twenty one years old he began to preach the Word in Newcastle Presbyterian Church. He was a very faithful minister of Christ, and saw many souls won to Christ.

In 1759 he was appointed President of Princeton as the successor of Jonathan Edwards. Samuel Davies died suddenly when only thirty six leaving behind a testimony to the grace of God seen in his short life of service.

As a hymn writer he is best known for his inspiring song: "Great God of wonders."

GREAT GOD OF WONDERS

Hymn 58 Tune: *Surrey* or *Sovereignty*

Great God of wonders! all Thy ways
 Display Thine attributes divine;
But the bright glories of Thy grace
 Above Thine other wonders shine:
Who is a pardoning God like Thee?
Or who has grace so rich and free?

Such deep transgressions to forgive!
 Such guilty, daring worms to spare!
This is Thy grand prerogative,
 And in this honour none shall share:
Who is a pardoning God like Thee?
Or who has grace so rich and free?

Pardon, from an offended God!
 Pardon, for sins of deepest dye!
Pardon, bestowed through Jesus' blood!
 Pardon, that brings the rebel nigh!
Who is a pardoning God like Thee?
Or who has grace so rich and free?

SAMUEL DAVIES

JAMES GEORGE DECK

Deck, James George (Bury St. Edmunds, England, Nov. 1, 1807—Motueka, New Zealand, August 14, 1884).

J.G. Deck was raised in the faith of the Church of England. As a young man he chose the army as a career. He trained at Paris, France under one of Napoleon's generals. In 1829 he was commissioned as an officer in the 14th Madras Regiment stationed in Bangalore, India. When on furlough in England he accepted the Lord Jesus as his Saviour. On his return to India he faithfully witnessed to his fellow officers. In 1835 he and his wife returned to England on account of his ill health. He became associated with other believers in the early days of the brethren movement. Later he resigned his commission and devoted himself to the preaching of the gospel in the villages of Devonshire, England. In 1852, due to failing health he and his family moved to New Zealand. There he laboured faithfully for the Lord for over thirty years. In 1882 he became a helpless invalid. Most of the twenty two hymns of J.G. Deck in the Believers Hymn Book were written in New Zealand. In 1985, when visiting New Zealand, the writer found that the fragrance of the life and testimony of John G. Deck was still known among the Lord's people. "The memory of the just is blessed" (Proverbs 10:7).

Abba, Father! we approach Thee 1
Around Thy grave, Lord Jesus 13
"A little while!" Our Lord shall come 14
He comes! Emmanuel comes! 68
Lamb of God! our souls adore Thee 122
Lamb of God! Thou now art seated 123
Lord Jesus, are we one with Thee? 128
Lord, we are Thine 143
Lord, we would ne'er forget Thy love 148
O Christ! we rest in Thee 175
O happy day! when first we felt 189
O Lamb of God! 'tis joy to know 196
O Lamb of God! still keep me 197
O Lord! 'tis joy to look above 199
O Lord, when we the path retrace 202
O Lord, who now art seated 205
O Thou Spotless Lamb of God 218
Saviour, Thy Name I love 245
The day of glory bearing 266
The veil is rent: Lo! Jesus stands 283
We bless our Saviour's Name 310
When first, o'erwhelmed with sin and shame 319

JAMES GEORGE DECK

SIR EDWARD DENNY, BART.

Denny, Sir Edward (Tralee, Ireland, Oct. 2, 1796—London, England, June 15, 1889).
Sir Edward Denny was the fourth baronet of Tralee Castle, Co. Kerry, Ireland. Though born to wealth and affluence, Sir Edward became interested in spiritual things in his early life. He became a devoted believer, and lived a long and fruitful life marked by humility and consecration to the Lord Jesus. He wrote many hymns which are all in the spirit of worship to God in appreciation of His Son, and in anticipation of His return. His finest selection of hymns was published in 1839. They are a precious legacy to the church. Most of these beautiful hymns are still in extensive use wherever saints assemble to remember the Lord in the "breaking of bread". One of his greatest and sweetest compositions is "To Calvary Lord, in spirit now, our weary souls repair".
Sir Edward was associated with brethren, who gathered in the Lord's Name, in the Gospel Hall, at Tralee, on his estate. He spent his closing years in Park Walk assembly in London, where he was called home in his ninety fourth year. His whole life was marked by grace and truth.

A PILGRIM THROUGH THIS LONELY WORLD

Hymn 11   Tune: *Lintone*

A Pilgrim through this lonely world
  The blessed Saviour passed;
A mourner all His life was He,
  A dying Lamb at last.

That tender heart that felt for all,
  For all its life-blood gave;
It found on earth no resting-place,
  Save only in the grave.

Such was our Lord, and shall we fear
  The cross with all its scorn?
Or love a faithless, evil world,
  That wreathed His brow with thorn?

Bright with all His crowns 31
Hope of our hearts, O Lord 75
O blessed Saviour, who but thou 174
O gracious Lord, be with us 183
O Lord, who art Thy people's light................... 198
O what a lonely path were ours 208
Sweet feast of love divine............................ 252
Tis finished all: our souls to win 303
Tis past, the dark and dreary night 304
To Calvary, Lord, in spirit now 305
What grace, O Lord, and beauty shone 316
While in sweet communion feeding 323
O wondrous hour, when Jesus, Thou.................. 433

SIR EDWARD DENNY, Bart.

WOLFGANG CHRISTOPHER DESZLER

Deszler, Wolfgang Christopher (Nurnberg, Germany, Feb. 11, 1660—Nurnberg, March 11, 1722).

W.C. Deszler had very poor health. On this account he had to give up his studies at the University of Altdorf. On his return to his home at Nurnberg he met a hymn writer, Erasmus Finx, who influenced him to write hymns. In a few years he had written over one hundred spiritual songs. He also composed music for all his hymns. These were published in 1692. Following a severe stroke Deszler suffered paralysis and six months later went to be with Christ. His best known hymn remains a favourite after more than two hundred years, and is included in the Believers Hymn Book.

O COME THOU STRICKEN LAMB OF GOD

Hymn 180   Tune: *Brynteg*

O come, Thou stricken Lamb of God!
Who shed'st for us Thine own life-blood,
And teach us all Thy love: then pain
Were sweet, and life or death were gain.

Take Thou our hearts, and let them be
For ever closed to all but Thee;
Thy willing servants, let us wear
The seal of love for ever there.

How blest are they who still abide
Close sheltered by Thy watchful side;
Who life and strength from Thee receive,
And with Thee move, and in Thee live!

WOLFGANG CHRISTOPHER DESZLER

MARIA DE FLEURY

De Fleury, Maria (London, England, 1743—London, 1794).
This devoted Christian composer co-authored some hymns with the well known hymn writer Dr. John Ryland, whose hymn "O Lord I would delight in Thee" is familiar to believers.

The hymns and spiritual songs of Maria De Fleury were published under the title *Poems on Spiritual Subjects* in 1781.

C.H. Spurgeon was impressed with her beautiful hymn "Thou softly flowing Kedron, 'twas by thy silver stream" and included it in his "Baptist Hymnal."

Another fine hymn "Come ye who bow to sovereign grace" is a short composition still used in gatherings of the Lord's people.

COME YE WHO BOW TO SOVEREIGN GRACE

Hymn 334   Tune: *Salway*

Come ye, who bow to sovereign grace,
   Record Immanuel's love;
Join in a song of grateful praise
   To Him who lives above.

Once in the gloomy grave He lay,
   But, by His rising power,
He bore the gates of death away:
   Hail! mighty Conqueror!

MARIA DE FLEURY

WILLIAM DICKINSON

Dickinson, William (London, England, 1816—1868).
William Dickinson was brought to faith in Christ as his Saviour and Lord in childhood. He was a faithful and devoted servant of Christ. When thirty years old he published a very interesting book *Hymns for Passion Week and the Forty Days*. These poems and hymns deal with events in the pathway of the Lord Jesus during His last week. The most remarkable being: "The Alabaster Box," "The Fig Tree," "The washing of the feet" and "Gethsemane." The last one is included in the Believers Hymn Book.

GETHSEMANE

Hymn 297   Tune: *Ezra*

'Twas love that sought Gethsemane,
  Or Judas ne'er had found Thee;
'Twas love that nailed Thee to the tree,
  Or iron ne'er had bound Thee.

'Twas love that lived, 'twas love that died,
  With endless life to bless us;
Well hast Thou won Thy blood-bought Bride,
  Worthy art Thou, Lord Jesus!

WILLIAM DICKINSON

PHILIP DODDRIDGE

Doddridge, Philip (London, England, June 20, 1702—Lisbon, Portugal, Oct. 6, 1751).

Philip Doddridge was the youngest child in a family of twenty. His father was an oil merchant, and his mother was the daughter of an exiled Christian, who had fled Bohemia because of severe persecution. His mother was a devoted Christian who read the Scriptures with her family. Philip trusted Christ as his Saviour while very young. A short time later both his parents died. When twenty years old he was invited to preach in St. Albans Independent Church. A number of his hearers were saved on this first occasion of his ministry. He was a very sick man most of his life, and finally was overtaken by consumption. Lady Huntington advised a change of climate, and sent him to Portugal. Two weeks after his arrival in Lisbon he died suddenly at the age of forty nine.

As a hymn writer, Doddridge is in the forefront. His four hundred compositions are both poetical and lyrical. Five of his hymns are included in the Believers Hymn Book, the best known being "O happy day that fixed my choice."

GRACE

Hymn 55   Tune: *Silchester*

Grace! 'tis a charming sound,
  Harmonious to the ear;
Heaven with the echo shall resound,
  And all the earth shall hear.

'Twas grace that wrote my name
  In life's eternal book;
'Twas grace that gave me to the Lamb,
  Who all my sorrows took.

Grace all the work shall crown
  Through everlasting days;
It lays in heaven the topmost stone,
  And well deserves the praise.

My God! what cords of love are Thine 154
O happy day that fixed my choice 188
Father of peace, and God of love 380
O God of Bethel! by whose hand 422

PHILIP DODDRIDGE

JOHN EAST

East, John. (Bath, England, 1793—1857).
John East was a minister of the Church of England at St. Michaels, Bath. He was noted for his faithful preaching of the Word of God. As a hymn writer he was well known by his three published hymn books. "There is a fold whence none can stray" was taken from one of these, titled "My Saviour."

THERE IS A FOLD

Hymn 279   Tune: *Lynnwood*

There is a fold whence none can stray,
   And pastures ever green,
Where sultry sun, or stormy day,
   Or night is never seen.

There is a Shepherd living there,
   The Firstborn from the dead,
Who tends with sweet, unwearied care
   The flock for which He bled.

There congregate the sons of light,
   Fair as the morning sky,
And taste of infinite delight
   Beneath their Saviour's eye.

JOHN EAST

K.H.
ELDERS

Elders, K.H.
 No data available.

Hymn 456   Tune: *Malvern*

The author of this beautiful hymn appreciated Christ as the Source of Peace, Life and Hope.

> Thou who did'st come to die
> From the bright realms on high,
>   Thou art our peace:
> Peace Thou dost now impart
> To each believing heart,
> Peace that shall ne'er depart;
>   Thou art our peace.
>
> Thou who did'st rise again,
> Thy tomb was sealed in vain,
>   Thou art our life:
> All power to Thee is given,
> Exalted Lord in heaven,
> And we with Thee are risen,
>   Thou art our life.
>
> Thou who wilt surely come
> To take Thy loved ones home,
>   Thou art our hope:
> What joys and bliss untold
> Will to our gaze unfold
> When we Thy face behold!
>   Thou art our hope.

K.H. ELDERS

JOHN ELLERTON

Ellerton, John (London, England, Dec. 16, 1826—Devon, England, June 15, 1893).

This writer occupies a place in the foremost rank of hymn-writers and hymnologists. He compiled and aided in the compilation of several hymnals. He is best known for his own compositions, many of which have a place in permanent collections. He was educated at Cambridge University and became a minister of the Church of England, preaching in Eastbourne and finally at Roding.

A sad note pervades Ellerton's hymns, but they are not less attractive on that account. He brings light into the darkest experiences of life. He wrote a large number of children's hymns, the most familiar being: "Again the morn of gladness." Two of his hymns are included in the Believers Hymn Book.

PARTING HYMN

Hymn 442   Tune: *Autumn*

Saviour, again to Thy dear name we raise
With one accord our parting hymn of praise:
We rise to bless Thee ere our worship cease;
Then, quietly waiting, hear Thy word of peace.

Grant us Thy peace upon our homeward way;
With Thee began, with Thee shall end the day;
Guard Thou the lips from sin, the hearts from shame,
That in this place have called upon Thy name.

Grant us Thy peace throughout our earthly life,
Our balm in sorrow and our stay in strife;
Then, when Thy voice shall bid our conflict cease,
Call us, O Lord, to Thine eternal peace.

The day Thou gavest, Lord, is ended 450

JOHN ELLERTON

CHARLOTTE ELLIOTT

Elliott, Charlotte (Brighton, England, March 18, 1789—Torquay, England, Sept. 22, 1871).

Charlotte Elliott was the third daughter of a family of six children. Although brought up in a Christian home she was over thirty years of age before she experienced conversion. In 1822 she was in a state of weakness through ill health, when Dr. Malan, an evangelist from Geneva was visiting her home. He questioned Charlotte regarding her salvation, which she resented and spoke in anger to Dr. Malan. Later, however, she apologised, and told him that she longed to know peace with God, but said she did not know how to come to Christ. Dr. Malan replied "Just come as you are." That evening she found peace and rest in the merits of the precious blood of Christ. For most of her life she was an invalid, often suffering great pain, and was seldom out of her room. In the quietness of her bedroom she wrote one of the most used and touching Gospel hymns of invitation ever composed: "Just as I am without one plea." Over one thousand letters were in the possession of Charlotte Elliott from souls who had been saved through this beautiful hymn.

MY GOD, MY FATHER, WHILE I STRAY

Hymn 165   Tune: *Magdale*

My God, my Father, while I stray
Far from my home, in life's rough way,
O teach me from my heart to say,
    "Thy will be done."

If dark my path and hard my lot,
May I be still and murmur not;
But breathe the prayer divinely taught
    "Thy will be done."

And when on earth I breathe no more
The prayer oft mixed with tears before,
I'll sing on heaven's blissful shore,
    "Thy will be done."

O Holy Saviour, Friend unseen 194
Just as I am, without one plea 333

CHARLOTTE ELLIOTT

DR. JOHN FOUNTAIN ELWIN

Elwin, John Fountain (Sicily, June 8, 1809—London, Nov. 17, 1890).

Dr. Fountain Elwin was the son of Col. Fountain Elwin of the British Army. Dr. Fountain Elwin became a Christian when studying for his M.D. at Cambridge University. He later became a world famous surgeon. In 1872 he was appointed Superintendent of the British Medical Mission, which he administered for fourteen years.

Dr. Fountain Elwin was a faithful witness and an acceptable preacher of the gospel. He also wrote a number of hymns published in "*The London Hymn Book.*" One of these is included in the Believers Hymn Book.

PEACE

Hymn 227   Tune: *Kirkby Bedon*

Peace! what a precious sound!
Tell it the world around;
　　Christ hath made peace!
Our souls are brought to God
By His atoning blood,
And crowned with every good;
　　Christ hath made peace!

Love was the spring of all,
Love triumphed o'er our fall,
　　The love of God!
My soul, this love adore,
And praise for evermore;
Yea, sound from shore to shore
　　The love of God!

Dr JOHN FOUNTAIN ELWIN

JAMES HARRINGTON EVANS

Evans, James Harrington (Salisbury, England, April 15, 1785—Stonehaven, Scotland, Dec. 1, 1849).

James H. Evans was the son of Dr. Evans of Salisbury. He was educated at Oxford university. It was there while a student that he trusted Christ as his Saviour. For many years he preached the Gospel faithfully in St. John Street Baptist Church in the city of London. In 1818 he published *Hymns for worship*. This contained one hundred and eighty hymns he had composed. One of his best known is a song of praise: "As sinners saved we gladly praise the Author of redeeming grace."

AS SINNERS SAVED

Hymn 12   Tune: *Duke St.*

As sinners saved we gladly praise
The Author of redeeming grace;
Father, 'tis Thine almighty power
Secures us when the tempests lower.

Thy love's a refuge ever nigh,
Thy watchfulness a mountain high,
Thy name a rock, which winds above
And waves below can never move.

Thy faithfulness, for ever sure,
Through endless ages shall endure;
Thy perfect work shall ever prove
The depth of Thine unceasing love.

While all things change, Thou changest not,
Forgetting ne'er, though oft forgot;
Thy love, immutably the same,
Displays the glory of Thy Name.

Lord, we would then rejoice and praise
The Source of all this wondrous grace;
Father, Thine everlasting power
Will keep us safe in danger's hour.

Faint not Christian.................................... 47

JAMES HARRINGTON EVANS

FREDERICK WILLIAM FABER

Faber, Frederick William (Calverley, Yorkshire, England, June 28, 1814—London, England, Sept. 26, 1863).

F.W. Faber was well educated gaining an honours degree at Oxford University. He had a strict Calvinistic background, but later under the influence of J.H. Newman became a follower of the Oxford Movement and entered the Roman Catholic Church.

Faber was a hymn-writer of note, composing one hundred and fifty hymns. "Faith of our Fathers, living still." is his best known.

One hymn is included in the Believers Hymn Book.

I BOW ME TO THY WILL, O GOD

Hymn 87   Tune: *Dunfermline*

I bow me to Thy will, O God,
  And all Thy ways adore,
And every day I live I'd seek
  To please Thee more and more.

He always wins who sides with God,
  To him no chance is lost;
God's will is sweetest to him when
  It triumphs at his cost.

Ill that God blesses is our good,
  And unblest good is ill;
And all is right that seems most wrong,
  If it be His sweet will.

FREDERICK WILLIAM FABER

MARIANNE FARNINGHAM

Farningham, Marianne (Farningham, Kent, England, Dec. 17, 1834—Northampton, England, March 16, 1909).

Marianne Farningham is the pseudonym for Marianne Hearn. Both her parents died while she was a child. She became a Christian early in life and began helping orphan children and homeless women in London. Dr. Whitemore, an influential journalist, saw her talent in writing poems and hymns, and sponsored her work. Marianne Farningham became the editor of *The Sunday School Times* and was the co-editor of the Christian newspaper *Christian World*.

Her complete literary works were published in twenty volumes. At the time of her death she was one of the most honoured women among Baptists in England. Her well known hymn, so suitable for the young Christian, is still in popular use, and is included in the Believers Hymn Book.

JUST AS I AM, THINE OWN TO BE

Hymn 405   Tune: *Cambridge* 8.8.8.6.

Just as I am, Thine own to be,
Friend of the young, who lovest me,
To consecrate myself to Thee,
 O Jesus Christ, I come.

In the glad morning of my day,
My life to give, my vows to pay,
With no reserve and no delay,
 With all my heart, I come.

Just as I am, young, strong and free,
To be the best that I can be
For truth, and righteousness, and Thee,
 Lord of my life, I come.

MARIANNE FARNINGHAM

JOHN FAWCETT

Fawcett, John (Bradford, England, Jan. 6, 1740—Hebden Bridge, England, July 25, 1817).

John Fawcett was converted through the preaching of George Whitefield at the age of sixteen. He became a Baptist preacher, ministering at Hebden Bridge for many years. Fawcett wrote many hymns of merit. The preface to his collection of hymns, published in 1782, reveals the authors evaluation of his work:

"I blush to think of these plain verses falling into the hands of persons of poetic genius. They were written to warm the hearts of God's people, and to produce devotion to the Person of the Lord Jesus Christ. If this is the outcome I will rejoice, whatever censure I may incur from the world."

John Fawcett was given an honorary D.D. degree from Brown University, Rhode Island, U.S.A. in 1811, for his *Commentary on the Holy Scriptures*. Two of his best known hymns are:

"Blest be the tie that binds" and "Lord dismiss us with Thy blessing."

DISMISSION

Hymn 132

Lord, dismiss us with Thy blessing,
   Fill our hearts with joy and peace;
Let us each, Thy love possessing,
   Triumph in redeeming grace;
     O refresh us
   Trav'lling through this wilderness.

Thanks we give and adoration
   For Thy gospel's joyful sound;
May the fruits of Thy salvation
   In our hearts and lives abound;
     Ever faithful
   To the truth may we be found.

So, whene'er the signal's given
   Us from earth to call away,
Upward borne by Thee to heaven,
   Glad the summons to obey,
     We shall ever
   Reign with Thee in endless day.

JOHN FAWCETT

WILLIAM RALPH FEATHERSTONE

Featherstone, William Ralph (Montreal, Canada, July 23, 1846—Montreal, May 20, 1873).

William Ralph Featherstone lived all his life in Montreal. His hymn "Lord Jesus I love Thee" has been ascribed to Adoniram J. Gordon, who acknowledged that he only composed the tune, having discovered the words in a monthly magazine.

Featherstone wrote this hymn after his conversion at the age of sixteen, and sent the words to his aunt in Los Angeles, whose godly influence had led him to trust the Lord Jesus.

His aunt was so impressed with the beautiful words of the hymn, she had it published in various Christian magazines, in 1862.

David Beattie in his book *Romance of Sacred Song* states that the original copy of the hymn is still a cherished treasure of the Featherstone family. The records are in St. James United Church in Montreal.

This unusual Canadian hymn writer went to be with the Lord, whom he loved, at the age of thirty three. His hymn is a favourite wherever believers gather for worship or ministry.

LORD JESUS I LOVE THEE

Hymn 134 Tune: *Jesus I love Thee* 11's

Lord Jesus, I love Thee, I know Thou art mine,
My rock and my fortress, my Surety divine;
My gracious Redeemer, my song shall be now,
'Tis Thou who art worthy, Lord Jesus, 'tis Thou!

I love Thee because Thou hast first lovèd me.
And purchased my pardon on Calvary's tree;
I love Thee for wearing the thorns on Thy brow;
'Tis Thou who art worthy, Lord Jesus, 'tis Thou!

And when the bright morn of Thy glory shall come,
And the children ascend to the Father's glad home,
I'll shout, with Thy likeness impressed on my brow,
'Tis Thou who art worthy, Lord Jesus, 'tis Thou!

WILLIAM RALPH FEATHERSTONE

ANNIE JOHNSTON FLINT

Flint, Annie Johnston (Vineland, N.J. U.S.A. 1866—Camden, N.J. 1932).

The great secret of the poems and hymns of Annie J. Flint was that she wrote from her heart as the result of the experiences of her life, the greater part of which was spent in pain and suffering, endured patiently. Her happy spirit showed how God could be glorified in the midst of physical trial. Left an orphan in poor circumstances at six years of age, she was adopted by a Christian couple in Camden, New Jersey. Before she was eight years old Annie trusted the Lord Jesus as her Saviour, and penned her first poem of praise when she was nine years of age. Arthritis became so severe that at twenty she was unable tc walk. For many years she continued to write beautiful poetry in which she ascribed honour to God and praise for His Son. Seven volumes of her works were published by the Evangelical Publishers, Toronto, Canada. From one of these the hymn "He giveth more grace" was chosen for the Believers Hymn Book. Shut in most of her life the hymns of Annie Johnston Flint are fragrant of heaven.

HE GIVETH MORE GRACE

Hymn 391   Tune: *Surrey* 12.11.12.11.

He giveth more grace when the burdens grow
  greater,
He sendeth more strength when the labours
  increase,
To added affliction He addeth His mercy,
  To multiplied trials His multiplied peace.

When we have exhausted our store of endurance,
  When strength has declined ere the day is
    half-done,
When we reach the end of our hoarded
    resources,
  Our Father's full giving is only begun.

His love has no limit, His grace has no measure,
  His power no boundary known unto men,
For out of His infinite riches in Jesus
  He giveth and giveth and giveth again.

ANNIE JOHNSTON FLINT

SAMUEL TREVOR FRANCIS

Francis, Samuel Trevor (Chesnut, Herts, England, Nov. 19, 1834—Kennington, England, Dec. 28, 1925).

Samuel Trevor Francis studied for the medical profession, but on the death of his father this was discontinued. At that time he came under soul trouble which led him to search the Scriptures for peace. He trusted Christ as his personal Saviour at the age of twenty three. Shortly afterwards he was baptised and associated with an assembly of Christians in London.

Francis wrote many beautiful hymns of outstanding merit. One of his greatest, "I am waiting for the dawning" is a hymn of anticipation of the coming again of the Lord Jesus for His Church. It is sung more than any other of the Second Advent hymns, and is a special favourite in assemblies of believers. It has been appropriately set to one of Franz Haydn's musical compositions. His hymn "Saviour, we remember Thee" is of great value when saints gather upon the Lord's Day to proclaim the Lord's Death.

Samuel Trevor Francis passed home to be with the Lord at the advanced age of ninety-one.

I AM WAITING FOR THE DAWNING

Hymn 81   Tune: *Austrian Hymn* 8.7.8.7.D.

I am waiting for the dawning
   Of the bright and blessèd day,
When the darksome night of sorrow
   Shall have vanished far away;
When for ever with the Saviour,
   Far beyond this vale of tears,
I shall swell the song of worship
   Through the everlasting years.

I am waiting for the coming
   Of the Lord who died for me;
O His words have thrilled my spirit,
   "I will come again for thee."
I can almost hear His footfall
   On the threshold of the door,
And my heart, my heart is longing
   To be with Him evermore.

Saviour, we remember Thee 251
Gracious God, we worship Thee 388
O the deep, deep love of Jesus 431

SAMUEL TREVOR FRANCIS

GEORGE WEST FRASER

Fraser, George West (Bally, Sligo, Ireland, 1830—Cheltenham, England, Jan. 24, 1896).

George West Fraser's father was the police inspector in the Royal Irish Constabulory in County Sligo. George Fraser was converted at twenty years of age listening to Gratton Guinness preach the Gospel in Dublin. Following his conversion he associated himself with Christians gathered to the Name of the Lord Jesus. He preached the Gospel faithfully for a number of years while still in the employ of the Bank of Ireland. Finally he resigned his position to devote all his time to the spread of the Gospel and the ministry of the Word in fellowship with assemblies of Christians.

George West Fraser wrote three volumes of hymns: *Midnight Praises, Day-Dawn Praises* and *Daystar Praises*. These are all of great spiritual value and of beautiful language. He also wrote the well known gospel hymn: "Come, hear the gospel sound." That he appreciated the Lord's Supper is fully evidenced in his hymn included in the Believers Hymn Book.

ON THAT SAME NIGHT, LORD JESUS

Hymn 435   Tune: *Eden Grove*, 7.6.7.6.D.

On that same night, Lord Jesus,
 In which Thou wast betrayed,
When without cause man's hatred
 Against Thee was displayed,
We hear Thy gracious accents—
 This do; remember Me;
With joyful hearts responding
 We would remember Thee.

We think of all the darkness
 Which round Thy spirit pressed,
Of all those waves and billows
 Which rolled across Thy breast;
'Tis there Thy grace unbounded
 And perfect love we see;
With joy and yet with sorrow
 We do remember Thee.

Till Thou shalt come in glory
 And call us hence away,
To share with Thee the brightness
 Of that unclouded day,
We show Thy death, Lord Jesus,
 And here would seek to be
More to that death conformèd
 Whilst we remember Thee.

GEORGE WEST FRASER

GORDON FURLONG

Furlong, Gordon (Parkhill, Aberdeen, Scotland, 1824—Rongotea, New Zealand, 31 August, 1908).

Gordon Furlong was named after his grandfather, who was General Gordon of Aberdeen. He was educated at Edinburgh University where he graduated as a lawyer. For some years he practised in this profession in Aberdeen. In 1851 he realised his need of salvation, and through reading the words of Lev. 17:11 "It is the blood that maketh atonement for the soul" he was saved. He soon associated himself with believers gathered in assembly fellowship in Aberdeen. Later he joined Brownlow North in the preaching of the gospel. Enormous crowds gathered to hear the two evangelists, and hundreds were saved in the cities, towns and villages of Scotland. The preaching of Gordon Furlong was solemn yet tender. Such well known brethren as John R. Caldwell (editor of the Witness), Alexander Marshall (author of the well known tract "God's way of salvation"), and C.H. Hinman (New Zealand), were brought to Christ through his ministry. He was also a student of the Scriptures and conducted many Bible Readings which were attended by such notable brethren as Lord Congleton and Harry Moorhouse.

In 1876 because of failing health he moved to New Zealand. His ministry in that land became a great blessing to the assemblies. As he became older his mental powers weakened, but he died in peace in Rongotea in 1908. Gordon Furlong had a large family all of whom were saved and in assembly fellowship. He was one of the outstanding evangelists of his generation. One hymn from his pen is included in the Believers Hymn Book. It was written soon after his conversion and evidences his value of the Precious Blood of Christ.

PRECIOUS IS THE BLOOD OF JESUS

Hymn 231   Tune: *Welsh Melody 1794*

Precious is the blood of Jesus
   Unto sinners who believe;
From the wrath of God it frees us,
   And salvation we receive:
      It is finished!
   Sounds with joy through earth and heaven.

Jesus now in heaven is seated,
   And by faith on Him we rest;
Soon the Church will be completed,
   And the saints with Him be blest:
      Grace and glory
   In our Saviour we receive.

Soon will pass the night of sorrow,
   And the Lord in glory come;
We shall see Him on the morrow,
   And the Bride be welcomed home:
      Hallelujah!
   Glory, glory to the Lamb!

GORDON FURLONG

SAMUEL WHITELOCK GANDY

Gandy, Samuel Whitelock (London, England, Dec. 24, 1851).
 Samuel Gandy was converted while very young. Even in childhood he manifested a spiritual mind and an unusual joy in the reading of the Scriptures. He entered the ministry of the Church of England and spent most of his life preaching in Kingston-on-Thames. His preaching was faithful and Christ-exalting in character. Many of his sermons were published posthumously in 1859. A selection of his hymns were also published entitled *Hymns of Gandy*. One of these known as "Victory through Christ" appeared first in *Hymns for the poor of the Flock*. This has been included in the Believers Hymn Book.

VICTORY THROUGH CHRIST

Hymn 93   Tune: *Serenity* S.M.

I hear the accuser roar
Of ills that I have done;
I know them well, and thousands more;
Jehovah findeth none.

There, in His book I bear
A more than conq'ror's name,
A soldier, son, and fellow-heir,
Who fought and overcame.

His be the Victor's name
Who fought our fight alone:
Triumphant saints no honour claim,
Their conquest was His own.

By weakness and defeat
He won the meed and crown;
Trod all our foes beneath His feet
By being trodden down.

Bless, bless the Conq'ror slain!
Slain in His victory!
Who lived, who died, who lives again,
For thee, His Church, for thee!

SAMUEL WHITELOCK GANDY

PAULUS GERHARDT

Gerhardt, Paulus (Grafinhainichen, Germany, March 12, 1606—Lubben, Germany, May 27, 1676).

Paulus Gerhardt wrote many hymns. He is described in the Encyclopedia Britannica as the greatest hymn writer of Germany. He was educated at the University of Wittenberg. During his early life he suffered much due to the disasters of the "Thirty Years War."

In 1642 he became a Christian. In Berlin he became a tutor in the home of a lawyer, Andreas Barthold. It was there that he was inspired to write devotional hymns concerning the Person of the Lord Jesus. He published *Cross and Comfort* which was translated into English by Catherine Winkworth. This book is highly commended. Much of Paulus Gerhardt's life was clouded with sorrow and tragedy. Four of his children died in infancy and his wife died after thirteen years of marriage. He also suffered unjustly from Frederick William the First of Saxony. In the Lutheran Church at Lubben there still remains a portrait of Gerhardt with this singular inscription: "*Theologus in cribo Satanas versatus.*" The meaning is "A Theologian sifted in Satan's sieve."

O HEAD, ONCE FILLED WITH BRUISES

Hymn 187   Tune: *Aurelia*

O Head, once filled with bruises,
    Oppressed with pain and scorn,
O'erwhelmed with sore abuses,
    Mocked with a crown of thorn!
O Head, to death once wounded
    In shame upon the tree,
In glory now surrounded
    With brightest majesty!

Thou Lord of all transcendent,
    Thou life-creating Sun
To worlds on Thee dependent,
    Yet bruised and spit upon!
O Lord! what Thee tormented
    Was our sin's heavy load;
We had the debt augmented,
    Which Thou didst pay in blood.

A Rock that stands forever 99
Midst the darkness, storm and sorrow 155
Put thou thy trust in God 440

PAULUS GERHARDT

ANNE TAYLOR GILBERT

Gilbert, Anne Taylor (London, England, Jan. 30, 1782—Nottingham, England, Dec. 20, 1866).

Anne Gilbert's father was an engraver by trade, but following his conversion he became an Independent preacher. She was brought to Christ in childhood. Her husband Joseph Gilbert was a faithful servant of Christ. Anne and her sister Jane published a hymnal suited for Sunday Schools. This book called *Hymns for Infant Minds* was popular both in England and the U.S.A. and was also translated into French and German. Anne Gilbert was very interested in the teaching of the Scriptures to the young and all her hymns were based upon the Word of God.

She is best remembered by her beautiful hymn which remains a favourite among believers, and is included in the Believers Hymn Book.

WHAT WAS IT, O OUR GOD

Hymn 354   Tune: *St. John*

What was it, O our God,
Led Thee to give Thy Son,
To yield Thy well-beloved
For us by sin undone?
'Twas love unbounded led Thee thus
To give Thy well-beloved for us.

What led the Son of God
To leave His throne on high,
To shed His pecious blood,
To suffer and to die?
'Twas love, unbounded love for us,
Led Him to die and suffer thus.

What love to Thee we owe,
Our God, for all Thy grace,
Our hearts should overflow
In everlasting praise:
Help us, O Lord, to praise Thee thus
For all Thy boundless love to us.

ANNE TAYLOR GILBERT

JOSEPH HENRY GILMOUR

Gilmour, Joseph Henry (Boston, U.S.A. April 29, 1834—Rochester, New York, July 23, 1918).

Joseph Henry Gilmour was Professor of Hebrew at Newton College. His father was the Governor of New Hampshire 1863-1864. During this time he worked as private secretary to his father, and also published the newspaper *Daily Monitor*. Later he was appointed as Dean of Rochester University, in which position he remained until retiring in 1911. He also published books on English and American literature which were used as text books in many universities. However he is best remembered by his beautiful hymn. Following a service in Philadelphia, where he was the guest speaker, he was constrained to write some words on the Shepherd of whom he had spoken from Psalm 23. In less than an hour he had completed the well known song of praise "He leadeth me, O blessed thought".

In 1926 the church where he had composed the hymn was demolished and an office building was erected by the Union Gas Company. On the front of that building is a Bronze Tablet paying tribute to the great hymn and its author, Joseph Henry Gilmour.

HE LEADETH ME

Hymn 70   Tune: *"Leadeth"*

He leadeth me, O blessed thought!
O words with heavenly comfort fraught!
Whate'er I do, where'er I be,
Still 'tis God's hand that leadeth me.
   He leadeth me! He leadeth me!
   By His own hand He leadeth me.

Sometimes 'mid scenes of deepest gloom,
Sometimes where Eden's bowers bloom,
By waters still, o'er troubled sea,
Still 'tis His hand that leadeth me.
   He leadeth me!

And when my task on earth is done,
When, by Thy grace, the vict'ry's won,
E'en death's cold wave I will not flee,
If God through Jordan leadeth me.
   He leadeth me!

JOSEPH HENRY GILMOUR

GEORGE GOODMAN

Goodman, George (London, England, 1866—London, 1942).
George Goodman was saved while a schoolboy. As a student at university he became interested in summer work with the Childrens Special Service Mission in bringing the gospel to children at holiday resorts. (The writer had the privilege of being present at one of his meetings in 1932.) George Goodman practised law in London for many years. Around 1924 he went forth to preach the Gospel in dependence upon the Lord, commended by the assembly of believers at Clapton Hall in London. God had given His servant gift to communicate the Word of God in an interesting manner, and he was much used in the salvation of young people. He wrote a number of books of great value to young Christians. One called *The Comforter* is a clear outline of the Person and work of the Holy Spirit. The hymns of George Goodman are indeed spiritual songs. Two of these are familiar in the gatherings of the Lord's people and are included in the Believers Hymn Book.

JESUS, LORD, I NEED THY PRESENCE

Hymn 399   Tune: *Ottawa*

Jesus, Lord, I need Thy presence
　As I journey on my way,
For without Thee I am lonely,
　And my feet are apt to stray;
But if Thou wilt walk with me
Life will calm and holy be.

Jesus, Lord, I need Thy wisdom,
　For perplexing problems press,
And without Thee I am foolish,
　Nor can bear the strain and stress;
But if Thou wilt counsel me
I shall true and upright be.

Jesus, Lord, Thy love so tender
　Is my greatest need of all,
For without Thee pride and anger
　From unguarded lips will fall;
But if Thou Thy love impart
I shall have a gracious heart.

The bread and wine are spread upon the board.........448

GEORGE GOODMAN

SIR ROBERT GRANT

Grant, Robert Sir (Bengal, India, 1779—Dalpoorie, India, July 9, 1838).

Sir Robert Grant was the son of Charles Grant a director of the East India Company. Robert Grant came under the influence of the gospel while a law student at Cambridge University. He became a believer in Christ, and remained faithful to God the rest of his life. He was called to the English Bar in 1807, and later became Judge Advocate General of England. In 1834 he was appointed Governor of Bombay, India, and was knighted.

Sir Robert Grant is best remembered by his great hymn: "O worship the King." His hymns were published posthumously by his brother Lord Glenelg in a book titled *Christian Psalmody*. This hymn received public acclaim when it appeared.

O WORSHIP THE KING

Hymn 434   Tune: *Hanover*

O worship the King all-glorious above,
O gratefully sing His power and His love;
Our shield and defender, the Ancient of Days,
Pavilioned in splendour and girded with praise.

O tell of His might, O sing of His grace,
  Whose robe is the light, whose canopy space;
His chariots of wrath the deep thunderclouds
    form,
And dark is His path on the wings of the storm.

The earth, with its store of wonders untold,
  Almighty, Thy power hath founded of old;
Hath stablished it fast by a changeless decree,
And round it hath cast, like a mantle, the sea.

SIR ROBERT GRANT

EMILY GRIMLEY

Grimley, Emily (Charleston, South Carolina, U.S.A. 1805—Philadelphia, 1879).

Emily Grimley and her sister Sarah were Quakers. They were saved in childhood and devoted themselves to the Lord. They worked for the abolition of slavery. After the death of their father, who as a wealthy landowner had many slaves, they set free all the family slaves. Because of the enmity against them by other slave masters they moved to Philadelphia. There they gave of their wealth to establish a sailors rest home where the social needs of sailors and their families could be met, but there was a strong emphasis on the Gospel and the spiritual welfare of men. The two sisters also visited hospitals and sought to bring the Gospel to outcast women on the streets of Philadelphia. They also opened a bookroom and distributed free copies of the New Testament. Emily Grimley wrote a number of spiritual hymns and poems. One of her best known is included in the Believers Hymn Book.

O WHAT SHALL WE FEEL IN THY PRESENCE

Hymn 225   Tune: *Security*

O what shall we feel in Thy presence when
    first
The visions of glory upon us shall burst!
Since now our soul longeth and seeketh for
    Thee;
O when, blessèd Saviour, Thy face shall we see?

That face, once so marred, we shall gaze on at
    length,
And fearless behold, as the sun in his strength;
Those eyes, flames of fire, that so searching we
    prove,
Shall beam on us then inexpressible love.

O Thou who this world as a lone pilgrim trod,
Thy Father our Father, Thy God is our God;
To Thee we behold the bright seraphim bow;
Lord Jesus, what glory doth rest on Thee
    now!

EMILY GRIMLEY

HENRY GRATTAN GUINNESS

Guinness, Henry Grattan (Montpellier, Ireland, Aug. 11, 1835—Dublin, Ireland, June 21, 1910).

Dr. Grattan Guinness was a man of outstanding personality, great energy, highly gifted, and full of devotion to the Lord Jesus Christ. His father was an officer in the Indian Army, and died when Henry and his brother were very young. The conversion of Robert had such an effect upon Henry that he turned from the world of pleasure in which he was engrossed and received Christ as his Lord and Saviour. He became associated with a company of believers near to his farm in Tipperary. A few years later he heard the call of God to serve Him fully in the gospel. He left his farm and lands and went forth depending alone upon God to supply his needs and guide his pathway. In Ireland he was greatly used in the revival of 1859. He also saw many saved in Scotland. He and his wife founded a college in Dubin where young men going forth into missionary work could have some preparation ministry. It is interesting to know that Hudson Taylor and Dr. Barnardo were among some of the brethren who received instruction from Dr. Guinness. Dr. Guinness was also a hymn writer of note. None of his compositions are so sacred and touching as the one included in the Believers Hymn Book.

CROWNED WITH THORNS

Hymn 42

Crowned with thorns upon the tree,
Silent in Thine agony;
Dying, crushed beneath the load
Of the wrath and curse of God.

On Thy pale and suff'ring brow,
Mystery of love and woe;
On Thy grief and sore amaze,
Saviour, I would fix my gaze!

On Thy pierced and bleeding breast
Thou dost bid the weary rest;
Rest there from the world's false ways,
Rest there from its vanities.

Sin-atoning Sacrifice,
Thou art precious in mine eyes;
Thou alone my rest shall be,
Now and through eternity.

HENRY GRATTAN GUINNESS

JOHN HAMPDEN GURNEY

Gurney, John Hampden (London, England, 1802—London 1862).
This writer was born into a wealthy family. His father was Sir John Gurney, a baron of the Court of the Exchequer. He was educated at Trinity College, Cambridge. Following his conversion, as a student, he entered the ministry of the Church of England. Later he became a Prebendary of St. Paul's Cathedral. He took a great interest in the distribution of tracts and was chairman of the Religious Tract Society. Dr. Gurney was a man of strong convictions yet of a tender spirit. He wrote a number of hymns of excellent quality; his greatest being: "We saw Thee not when Thou didst come." This beautiful spiritual song is a favourite among Christians.

WE SAW THEE NOT WHEN THOU DIDST COME

Hymn 461　　Tune: *Pater Omnium*

We saw Thee not when Thou didst come
To this poor world of sin and death,
Nor e'er beheld Thy cottage home
In that despisèd Nazareth;
But we believe Thy footsteps trod
Its streets and plains, Thou Son of God.

We did not see Thee lifted high
Amid that wild and savage crew,
Nor heard Thy meek, imploring cry,
Forgive, they know not what they do;
Yet we believe the deed was done
Which shook the earth, and veiled the sun.

We stood not by the empty tomb
Where late Thy sacred body lay,
Nor sat within that upper room,
Nor met Thee in the open way;
But we believe the angel said,
Why seek the living with the dead?

We did not mark the chosen few
When Thou didst through the clouds ascend,
First lift to heaven their wondering view,
Then to the earth all prostrate bend;
Yet we believe that mortal eyes
Beheld that journey to the skies.

JOHN HAMPDEN GURNEY

JANE E. HALL

Hall Jane E. (Vermont, U.S.A. 1834—Battlefield, U.S.A. 1896).

Jane Hall was saved in childhood. Her greatest contribution to hymnody "The love that Jesus had for me" was first used by Ira D. Sankey and was included in "Sacred Songs and Solos."

Fifty million of this hymnal have been sold.

Jane Hall composed the appropriate tune which has contributed to the beauty of the hymn in its continued popularity.

No other hymn is ascribed to the writer, but this one has been widely used in the blessing of souls and the promotion of thanksgiving to God for His Well-Beloved Son, whose love is more than tongue can tell.

MORE THAN TONGUE CAN TELL

Hymn 282

The love that Jesus had for me,
To suffer on the cruel tree
That I a ransomed soul might be,
　Is more than tongue can tell!

　His love is more than tongue can tell!
　His love is more than tongue can tell!
　The love that Jesus had for me
　　Is more than tongue can tell!

The many sorrows that He bore,
And O, that crown of thorns He wore,
That I might live for evermore,
　Is more than tongue can tell!

JANE E. HALL

EDWARD PAYSON HAMMOND

Hammond, Edward Payson (Ellington, Conn. U.S.A. Sept. 1, 1831—Bridgeport, Conn. 1910).

Edward Payson Hammond became a Christian at the age of seventeen. When he was twenty he went forth to evangelise and preached in many parts of New England, where God used him in the salvation of a great number of precious souls. He compiled a useful Gospel Hymn Book for special use in evangelistic services. Edward Hammond wrote a few very spiritual songs, but the one included in the Believers Hymn Book is a well known missionary hymn, often sung in the assemblies of Christians.

CHRISTIANS, GO AND TELL OF JESUS

Hymn 35   Tune: *Beautiful River*

Christians, go and tell of Jesus,
　How He died to save our souls;
How that He, from sin might free us,
　Suffered agonies untold.

　　Yes, we'll go and tell of Jesus,
　　　The pure and holy, meek and lowly
　　　　Jesus;
　　Yes, we'll go and tell of Jesus,
　　　Who died our souls to save.

Tell them of the joys of heaven,
　Purchased by the Saviour's blood;
How, that they might be forgiven,
　Jesus left His home above.

Tell them how He hath ascended
　To prepare a home on high,
Where all sorrows shall be ended,
　Where the saved shall never die.

EDWARD PAYSON HAMMOND

WILLIAM HAMMOND

Hammond, William (Sussex, England, 1719—London, England, 1783).

William Hammond was saved in his early life. He graduated from Cambridge University, where he was an honours student in all subjects.

As one of the Moravian Brethren his hymns rank with James Montgomery and John Cennick. The hymns of William Hammond were published as *Psalms, Hymns and Spiritual Songs*. In the preface he wrote of his full assurance of faith and of his joy in the Person and work of the Lord Jesus Christ.

Some of his hymns have attained a foremost place in the realm of English hymnody. He also translated many Latin hymns which were among the earliest to be published. Dr. Julian states that these are of outstanding merit and worthy of attention.

AWAKE AND SING THE SONG

Hymn 368   Tune: *Carlisle*

Awake, and sing the song
Of glory to the Lamb!
Wake every heart and every tongue
To praise the Saviour's name.

Sing of His dying love,
Sing of His rising power,
Sing how He intercedes above
For those whose sins He bore.

Soon shall we hear Him say,
Ye blessèd children, come;
Soon will He call us hence away,
And take us to His home.

There shall each raptured tongue
His endless praise proclaim;
And sweeter voices tune the song
Of glory to the Lamb.

WILLIAM HAMMOND

JOSEPH HART

Hart, Joseph (London, England, 1712—Bunhill Fields, England, May 24, 1768).

Joseph Hart had a Christian background. He had a good education and was headmaster in a village school. For many years he lived a careless and sinful life. However a notable miracle was known when he was forty five years of age in God's dealings with him concerning his soul's salvation. His indifference gave way to deep concern about his lost estate and the danger of going to hell. After weeks of soul trouble he finally rested upon the merits of the Saviour's death for him at Calvary. His life was changed and his evident gift to preach the gospel was acknowledged by all who heard his faithful presentation of the Truth. Many souls were saved through his untiring labours during the eleven years of his short Christian life. His efforts as a hymn-writer placed him as a valuable contributor to English hymnody. His best known gospel song is "Come ye sinners, poor and wretched". "How good is the God we adore" is included in the Believers Hymn Book, and is still widely used.

This notable servant of Christ died suddenly in his fifty seventh year. It was estimated that over twenty thousand people attended his burial, which was the largest ever witnessed in that part of England. The large congregation sang his own hymn "How good is the God we adore" around his graveside.

HOW GOOD IS THE GOD WE ADORE

Hymn 78   Tune: *Tabor*

How good is the God we adore,
Our faithful, unchangeable Friend,
Whose love is as great as His power,
   And knows neither measure nor end!

'Tis Jesus, the First and the Last,
   Whose Spirit shall guide us safe home;
We'll praise Him for all that is past,
   And trust Him for all that's to come.

Once more before we part..........................211

This hymn was written by Joseph Hart in two stanzas. Twenty five years later Dr. Robert Hawker of Exeter added a further verse and chorus.

JOSEPH HART

FRANCES RIDLEY HAVERGAL

Havergal, Frances Ridley (Astley, England, Dec. 14, 1836—Swansea, S. Wales, June 3, 1878).
This author began writing when she was eight years old. Her first poems appeared in the magazine *Good Words*. Her whole life was one of frail and delicate health. God gave her a wonderful ability. She could speak fluently seven languages, and was also a Greek and Hebrew scholar. At the age of fourteen she became a Christian. All her hymns reflect the joy of this experience and her consecration to the Saviour as Lord of her life.

The best loved hymn of Francis Havergal "Take my life and let it be, ever only Lord for Thee" has been translated into thirty languages. At the early age of forty two she passed into the presence of the One of whom she sang: "Thy life was given for me, Thy blood, O Lord, was shed."

Six of her hymns are included in the Believers Hymn Book.

TAKE MY LIFE

Hymn 446 Tune: *Lubeck*

Take my life, and let it be
Consecrated, Lord, to Thee;
Take my moments and my days,
Let them flow in ceaseless praise.

Take my voice, and let me sing
Always, only, for my King;
Take my lips, and let them be
Filled with messages from Thee.

Take my will, and make it Thine,
It shall be no longer mine;
Take my heart—it is Thine own,
It shall be Thy royal throne.

Take my love; my Lord, I pour
At Thy feet its treasure-store:
Take myself, and I will be
Ever, only, all for Thee.

Thou art coming, O our Saviour 288
Like a river, glorious is God's perfect peace 407
Lord, speak to me, that I may speak 410
Master, speak! Thy servant heareth 415
Thy life was given for me 458

FRANCES RIDLEY HAVERGAL

DR. THOMAS HAWEIS

Haweis, Thomas (Truro, England, 1732—Bath, 1820).
Thomas Haweis was born into an aristocratic family. He was well educated and obtained a M.D. degree at Oxford University. He became a Christian through the faithful preaching of the Church of England minister at Truro. At the age of twenty five he entered the ministry and became a curate in Oxford. Because of his evangelistic preaching the Bishop of Oxford ousted him from his position. At that time he became associated with other Christians who gathered together for Bible study in the mansion of Selina Shirley, the Countess of Huntingdon. He there met with such hymn-writers as Toplady and the Wesleys. The countess encouraged Dr. Haweis to write hymns. He became a prolific writer and had two hundred of his compositions published. Two of these are preserved in the Believers Hymn Book. Dr. Thomas Haweis was a faithful and devoted servant of Christ.

LORD JESUS TO TELL OF THY LOVE

Hymn 142   Tune: *David*

Lord Jesus, to tell of Thy love,
Our souls shall for ever delight,
And join with the blessèd above
In praises by day and by night.

Wherever we follow Thee, Lord,
Admiring, adoring, we see
That love which was stronger than death
Flow out without limit, and free.

Descending from glory on high,
With men Thy delight was to dwell;
Contented, our Surety to die,
By dying to save us from hell.

Enduring the grief and the shame,
And bearing our sins on the Cross,
O who would not boast of Thy love,
And count the world's glory but dross!

The happy morn is come 268

Dr. THOMAS HAWEIS

DR. ROBERT HAWKER

Hawker, Robert (Exeter, England, 1753—Plymouth, 1827).
Robert Hawker obtained his M.D. at Oxford University. He was converted at the age of twenty five and became a faithful preacher of the gospel in Plymouth and the surrounding villages for the rest of his life. Many were led to Christ through his plain presentation of the Truth. Dr. Hawker wrote five hymns, two of which are included in the Believers Hymn Book.

His hymns bring the preciousness of the Lord Jesus into focus, and their language is immeasurably beautiful.

The well known hymn "Once more before we part" was originally written by Joseph Hart in 1762. Twenty five years later Dr. Hawker added another verse and the chorus. Dr. Robert Hawker also published an interesting collection of Sunday School hymns.

ABBA FATHER, WE ADORE THEE

Hymn 2　　　Tune: *Old 42nd*

Abba, Father! we adore Thee,
　　Humbly now our homage pay:
'Tis Thy children's bliss to know Thee,
　　Welcomed through the living way:
This high honour we inherit,
　　Thy free gift through Jesus' blood;
God the Spirit, with our spirit,
　　Witnesseth we're sons of God.

Thine own purpose gave us being,
　　When, in Christ, in that vast plan
Thou in Christ didst choose Thy people
　　E'en before the world began:
O what love the Father bore us!
　　O how precious in Thy sight!
When Thou gav'st Thy Church to Jesus,
　　Jesus, Son of Thy delight.

Dr. ROBERT HAWKER

REGINALD HEBER

Heber, Reginald (Cheshire, England, April 21, 1783—Trichinopoly, India, April 3, 1826).
Reginald Heber has an important place in the realm of hymnology. He was born into wealth and affluence. His father was the Lord of Marton Manor, Yorkshire. Heber was converted to God as a student at Oxford University. He was possessed of a kind disposition, a prayerful spirit, a tender compassion, and great devotion to Christ.

For many years he preached in Hodnet, Shropshire, where many were saved through His faithful ministry. In 1823 he accepted the appointment as Bishop of Calcutta, India, but he only lived three years in India. He was found by his servant dead in his bath, stricken with apoplexy. He had an honourable burial in India. Two great hymns came from his pen: "From Greenland's icy mountains" and "Holy, Holy, Holy, Lord God Almighty." It is said by leading hymnologists that these two hymns are found in more hymn books than any other ever written.

HOLY, HOLY, HOLY

Hymn 392   Tune: *Nicaea*

Holy, holy, holy! Lord God Almighty!
  Early in the morning our song shall
    rise to Thee;
Holy, holy, holy! merciful and mighty,
  God in Three Persons, blessèd Trinity!

Holy, holy, holy! though the darkness hide
    Thee,
Though the eye of sinful man Thy glory may
    not see;
Only Thou art holy, there is none beside Thee,
  Perfect in power, in love, and purity.

Holy, holy, holy! Lord God Almighty!
All Thy works shall praise Thy name in earth,
    and sky, and sea;
Holy, holy, holy! merciful and mighty.
  God in Three Persons, blessèd Trinity!

From Greenland's icy mountains..................382

REGINALD HEBER

ELIZA EDMUNDS HEWITT

Hewitt, Eliza Edmunds (Philadelphia, U.S.A. June 28, 1851—Philadelphia, April 24, 1920).

Eliza Hewitt was the daughter of Captain James Stites. She had a good education and graduated a Valedictorian of her grade. She became a school teacher. At the age of twenty she accepted Christ as her Saviour and Lord. She had a God given gift among young people and gathered large numbers to her home where she conducted children's meetings for many years. In the realm of hymnody she holds an honoured place on account of her two greatest hymns: "Sing the wondrous love of Jesus" and "More about Jesus would I know."

Her over one hundred hymns were published by Homer Rodeheaver. "More about Jesus" has an appropriate tune composed by John R. Sweeney and is a favourite of Christians everywhere.

MORE ABOUT JESUS

Hymn 418   Tune: *More about Jesus*

More about Jesus would I know,
More of His grace to others show;
More of His saving fulness see,
More of His love who died for me.

    More, more about Jesus,
    More, more about Jesus;
    More of His saving fulness see,
    More of His love who died for me.

More about Jesus let me learn,
More of His holy will discern;
Spirit of God, my teacher be,
Showing the things of Christ to me.

More about Jesus; on His throne,
Riches in glory all His own;
More of His kingdom's sure increase;
More of His coming—Prince of Peace.

ELIZA EDMUNDS HEWITT

MARY JANE HOARE

Hoare, Mary Jane (1840—).
Very little information is obtainable about this author. The hymn "The night is wearing fast away" first appeared anonymously in the early brethren Hymn Book *Hymns for the Poor of the Flock* 1838. In *The Christian Hymn Book* it is attributed to Sir Edward Denny, but it is not included in the complete hymns of Denny published in 1870.

J. Denham Smith published a hymnal *Times of Refreshing* and there the author's name is given as "Hoare".

The delightful hymn is one of the Second Advent hymns included in the Believers Hymn Book.

THE NIGHT IS WEARING FAST AWAY

Hymn 278   Tune: *Bishopgarth*

The night is wearing fast away,
  The glorious day is dawning,
When Christ shall all His grace display,
  The fair millennial morning.
Gloomy and dark the night hath been,
  And long the way, and dreary;
And sad the weeping saints are seen,
  And faint, and worn, and weary.

Ye mourning pilgrims, dry your tears,
  And hush each sigh of sorrow;
The light of that bright morn appears,
  The long Sabbatic morrow.
Lift up your heads! behold from far
  A flood of splendour streaming!
It is the bright and Morning Star,
  In living lustre beaming.

MARY JANE HOARE

ERNST CHRISTOPH HOMBURG

Homburg, Ernst Christoph (Mihla, Germany, 1605—Naumberg, 1681).

Ernst Christoph Homburg was the Clerk of Assizes at Naumberg, Germany. In spite of his position of responsibility he spent many years in producing debased love songs and drunken songs, which characterised the age in which he lived. He was a poet of talent but all was used in the evil ways of sin. He was stricken with a severe plague and in deep distress he turned to God in true repentance and cried for mercy. God heard his cry and raised him up, and Homburg trusted Christ as his Saviour and Lord. From that day he served the Lord faithfully and used his pen and all his ability to bring praise, honour and glory to God and His Well-Beloved Son. Many were saved through his testimony. One of his greatest hymns "Jesus, Source of Life Eternal" was translated from German to English over two hundred years after it was written. The translater was Hannah Burlington. This beautiful hymn is included in the Believers Hymn Book.

JESUS! SOURCE OF LIFE ETERNAL

Hymn 115   Tune: *Whither? Pilgrims*

Jesus! Source of life eternal,
  Jesus! Author of our breath
Victor o'er the hosts infernal
  By defeat, and shame, and death.
Thou through deepest tribulation
Deigned to pass for our salvation:
  Thousand, thousand praises be,
  Lord of Glory, unto Thee.

Thou, O Son of God, wert bearing
  Cruel mockings, hatred, scorn;
Thou, the King of Glory, wearing,
  For our sake, the crown of thorn:
Dying, Thou didst us deliver
From the chains of sin for ever:
  Thousand, thousand praises be,
  Precious Saviour, unto Thee.

ERNST CHRISTOPH HOMBURG

HENRY JOY McCRACKEN HOPE

Hope, Henry Joy McCracken (Belfast, Nth. Ireland, 1809—Dunadry, Co. Antrim, Nth. Ireland, Jan. 19, 1872).

Henry Joy McCracken Hope was the son of James Hope, and was a book binder to trade. He was employed by the firm of Chambers in Dublin for many years. In Dublin he was brought under the sound of the Gospel and came to Christ for salvation. His life was changed and he witnessed faithfully to all with whom he came in contact in business.

Shortly after his conversion he wrote one hymn that has been preserved "Now I have found a Friend". It was printed in 1852 under the title "Jesus the Friend". Philip Bliss composed the tune to which the hymn is sung.

Henry Hope retired to Dunadry and is buried there. On his tombstone the words were graven—his own words "Farewell mortality, Jesus is mine, welcome eternity, Jesus is mine."

JESUS IS MINE

Hymn 168   Tune: *Feast*

Now I have found a Friend,
    Jesus is mine;
His love shall never end,
    Jesus is mine;
Though earthly joys decrease,
Though human friendships cease,
Now I have lasting peace,
    Jesus is mine.

Though I grow poor and old,
    Jesus is mine;
He will my faith uphold,
    Jesus is mine;
He will my wants supply,
His precious blood is nigh,
Nought can my hope destroy,
    Jesus is mine.

Farewell, mortality!
    Jesus is mine;
Welcome, eternity!
    Jesus is mine.
He my redemption is,
Wisdom and righteousnesss,
Life, light, and holiness,
    Jesus is mine.

HENRY JOY McCRACKEN HOPE

JOSEPH HOSKINS

Hoskins, Joseph (London, England, 1745—1788).

Joseph Hoskins was saved in childhood reading the words "Behold the Lamb of God" (John 1:29). He became an Independent minister, and for ten years preached the gospel with great blessing around Bristol, England. He went to be with Christ at the early age of forty three. During his last three years he authored over four hundred hymns. These were published by Moody and Bottomly under the title "Devotional Subjects for Singing" in 1788.

The hymns of Hoskins have little poetic merit, but are full of great spiritual truths.

The one included in the Believers Hymn Book is frequently used in the gatherings of the Lord's People.

BEHOLD! BEHOLD THE LAMB OF GOD

Hymn 30   Tune: *On the Cross*

Behold! behold the Lamb of God,
  On the Cross!
For us He shed His precious blood,
  On the Cross.
O hear His all-important cry,
"Eli, lama sabachthani?"
Draw near and see the Saviour die
  On the Cross!

Behold His arms extended wide,
  On the Cross!
Behold His bleeding hands and side,
  On the Cross!
The sun withholds its rays of light,
The heav'ns are clothed in shades of night,
While Jesus wins the glorious fight,
  On the Cross!

And now the mighty deed is done,
  On the Cross!
The battle fought, the vict'ry won,
  On the Cross!
To heav'n He turns His languid eyes,
"'Tis finished" now, the Conqueror cries,
Then bows His sacred head and dies,
  On the Cross!

JOSEPH HOSKINS

AMELIA MATILDA HULL

Hull, Amelia Matilda (Marpole, England, 1825—Exmouth, 1882).

Amelia Matilda Hull was born into a Christian home. Her brother Captain Hull was a notable person in the early days of the brethren movement. She came to Christ for salvation as a girl and lived her life in devotion and self sacrifice for the Lord.

Her greatest contribution to hymnody is the well known gospel hymn "There is life for a look at the crucified One", which has gained world wide acceptance.

H.W. Soltau published her hymns and highly commended their spiritual content. She wrote her hymn "I have been at the altar" for use by Soltau in his lectures on the Tabernacle, the Priesthood and the Offerings.

I HAVE BEEN AT THE ALTAR

Hymn 88   Tune: *It is Well*

I have been at the altar and witnessed the Lamb
  Burnt wholly to ashes for me;
And watched its sweet savour ascending on high,
  Accepted, O Father, by Thee.

And lo, while I gazed at the glorious sight,
  A voice from above reached mine ears:
"By this thine iniquity's taken away,
  And no trace of it on thee appears."

O Lord, I believe it with wonder and joy;
  Confirm, Thou, this precious belief;
While daily I learn that I am, in myself,
  Of sinners the vilest and chief.

AMELIA MATILDA HULL

CHARLES RUSSELL HURDITCH

Hurditch, Charles Russell (Exeter, England, Dec. 20, 1839—London, 1908).
This author was converted when fifteen years of age. He became an ardent soul winner, commencing in the villages of Devonshire. Later he was appointed secretary of the Y.M.C.A. at its London headquarters. At that time the Y.M.C.A. was a thriving evangelical movement. Charles Russell Hurditch published and distributed over sixteen million tracts in his lifetime. He also published the magazine *Footsteps of the Flock*. He wrote twenty seven hymns, which are all characterised by great simplicity and spiritual depth. Four of his best hymns are included in the Believers Hymn Book.

O CHRIST THOU HEAVENLY LAMB

Hymn 179   Tune: *Swabia*

O Christ, Thou heavenly Lamb!
Joy of the Father's heart;
Now let Thy love my soul inflame,
Fresh power to me impart.

Power to know the loss
Suffered, O Lord, by Thee;
Power to glory in the Cross
Thou didst endure for me.

Power lost souls to win
From Satan's mighty hold;
Power the wanderers to bring
Back to the heavenly fold.

Power to watch and pray,
"Lord Jesus, quickly come!"
Power to hail the happy day
Destined to bear me home.

Rejoice! rejoice, ye saints rejoice 237
Farewell, for the present, farewell 358
He dies! He dies! the lowly Man of Sorrows............. 390

CHARLES RUSSELL HURDITCH

JAMES HUTTON

Hutton, James (London, England, Sept. 13, 1715—Chelsea, England, May 3, 1795).

This hymn writer was a cousin of Sir Isaac Newton. He was the owner of a large bookstore in the inner city of London. As a young man he was converted through listening to Charles Wesley preach the gospel in the open air. His bookshop became a meeting place of believers and also in a large room upstairs he had gospel meetings every week. When Hutton visited Herrnhut, a Moravian settlement in Moravia, Germany and met Count Zinzendorf the founder of the group, he was so influenced by their godly ways and devotion to the Person of Christ that he cast in his lot with them, enjoying their fellowship the rest of his life.

In 1741 he printed the Moravian Hymn Book and contributed several hymns which he had authored. The grandest of all his hymns is still often sung whenever Christians assemble for the ministry of the Word of God. This beautiful hymn of prayer "O teach us more of Thy blest ways" is included in the Believers Hymn Book.

O TEACH US MORE OF THY BLEST WAYS

Hymn 195 Tune: *Eden*

O teach us more of Thy blest ways,
　Thou holy Lamb of God!
And fix and root us in Thy grace,
　As those redeemed by blood.

O tell us often of Thy love,
　Of all Thy grief and pain!
And let our hearts with joy confess
　That thence comes all our gain.

Engrave this deeply on our heart,
　Conform our ways to Thine,
That so we may, in some degree,
　Reflect the light divine.

JAMES HUTTON

WINIFRED A. IVERSON

Iverson, Winifred A.
   Concerning this writer we have no available information at this time. Her beautiful poem which is sung as a hymn has brought joy and peace to many tried saints, and renewed confidence in the perfect purpose of all God's ways.

THE LORD WILL PERFECT THAT WHICH DOTH CONCERN ME

Hymn 453

The Lord will perfect that which doth
　concern me,
His way is perfect, so His goal must be;
All life's events in harmony are working
　For those clear issues which I yet shall see.

The Lord will perfect that which doth concern
　me,
　And will complete each half-formed thing
　　He sends:
His rich designs most carefully are woven,
　There are with Him no loose or broken ends.

The Lord will perfect that which doth concern
　me,
　And finish what His grace has here begun;
He gathers up life's fragments, losing
　　nothing,
　And turns to good account each single one.

WINIFRED A. IVERSON

GEORGE
JEKEL

Jekel, George (Lanarkshire, Scotland, Jan. 17, 1804—Perth, Feb. 15, 1892).
George Jekel was converted in childhood. He graduated from Glasgow University and became a preacher in Auchterarder in Perthshire, Scotland. He preached the Word of God faithfully and was known for His godly manner of life. He published two books of poems and hymns: *The Clouds* in 1866 and *The Hope* in 1875. In both of these he emphasised the second coming of the Lord. It is interesting to note that he believed in the Rapture of the Church at any moment, to precede the Revelation of Christ as the King. His beautiful hymn "Lord Jesus, Come! and take Thy people Home" has brought comfort and hope to many believers.

LORD JESUS, COME!

Hymn 130   Tune: *Patience*

Lord Jesus, come!
Nor let us longer roam
Afar from thee, and that bright place
Where we shall see Thee face to face.
Lord Jesus, come!

Lord Jesus, come!
Thine absence here we mourn;
No joy we know apart from Thee,
No sorrow in Thy presence see.
Come, Saviour, come!

Lord Jesus, come!
And take Thy people home;
That all Thy flock, so scattered here,
With Thee in glory may appear.
Lord Jesus, come!

GEORGE JEKEL

RICHARD KEENE

Keene, Richard (—1787).

The well known hymn "How firm a foundation" first appeared in a collection published by Dr. John Rippon, a Baptist minister, in 1787. There has always been a mystery concerning the author. The only designation to the hymn is the letter "K". The hymn has been ascribed to Dr. Rippon by some, and to a George Keith by others. However Dr. John Julian, who is one of the most reliable authorities in the realm of hymnology fixes the origin of the hymn to Richard Keene, who was the precentor in Dr. Rippon's congregation.

The beautiful hymn is of great spiritual value. The last stanza has a powerful and affecting emphasis on the Divine promise (Hebrews 13:5).

"The soul that on Jesus hath leaned for repose,
He will not, He cannot desert to its foes;
That soul, though all hell should endeavour to shake,
He'll never—no, never—no, never forsake!"

HOW FIRM A FOUNDATION YE SAINTS OF THE LORD

Hymn 77   Tune: *Montgomery*

How firm a foundation, ye saints of the Lord,
Is laid for your faith in His excellent Word!
What more can He say, than to you He hath said,
You who to the Saviour for refuge have fled?

Fear not, He is with thee; oh, be not dismayed!
He—He is thy God, and will still give thee aid;
He'll strengthen thee, help thee, and cause thee to stand,
Upheld by His righteous, omnipotent hand.

RICHARD KEENE

THOMAS KELLY

Kelly, Thomas (Kellyville, Athy, Ireland, July 13, 1769—Dublin, Ireland, May 14, 1855).

Authorities are agreed that Ireland has never furnished a greater or more prolific hymn-writer than Thomas Kelly. He wrote 765 hymns published in Dublin in 1802 under the title *A Collection of Hymns*. Thomas Kelly was educated at Trinity College Dublin as a lawyer. However thoughts of eternal matters caused him to seek salvation, and after a considerable time of soul trouble he was led to the Lord Jesus, to rest upon the merits of His precious blood. In 1792 he was ordained in the Church of England, but because of his faithful preaching of the gospel, the Archbishop of Dublin closed all pulpits in the diocese to Kelly. He henceforth went forth as an independent evangelist. Being an attractive preacher and a man of great wealth, he devoted his energies to helping the poor peasants, and forming congregations of believers. Thomas Kelly was a musician and composed music for over 700 of his own hymns. The Believers Hymn Book has included 19 of these hymns. Mr. W.E. Vine states of his hymns: "The hymns of Thomas Kelly direct the heart immediately to the worship of God, and to heart occupation with the Father, and with His Son Jesus Christ, and are of pre-eminent value in the realm of spiritual hymnody." In 1854, he had a severe stroke while preaching the gospel, but lingered for a year. He was called home in his 87th year.

BEHOLD THE LAMB WITH GLORY CROWNED

Hymn 17   Tune: *St. Magnus*

Behold the Lamb with glory crowned!
  To Him all power is given;
No place too high for Him is found,
  No place too high in heaven.

He fills the throne—the throne above,
  He fills it without wrong;
The object of His Father's love,
  The theme of angels' song.

Crowns of glory ever bright 44
Glory, glory everlasting............................... 52
Glory to God on high 56
Happy they who trust in Jesus 62
Lord, accept our feeble song.......................... 126
Look, ye saints, the sight is glorious 127
Meeting in the Saviour's Name........................ 149
Praise the Lord, who died to save us.................. 232
Praise the Saviour, ye who know Him 233
Saviour, through the desert lead us................... 254
The atoning work is done 260
The Head that once with thorns was bound 269
The Lord is risen 275
The night is far spent................................ 284
We sing the praise of Him who died................... 315
We'll sing of the Shepherd that died 318
Endless praises to our Lord........................... 336
God is love! His word hath said it 357

THOMAS KELLY

THOMAS KEN

Ken, Thomas (Berkhamstead, England, July 1637—Longleat, March 19, 1711).

Thomas Ken's parents died when he was a child. His half-sister Anne Walton brought him up. He was educated at Oxford and became a curate in Winchester. His preaching was marked by great faithfulness, causing him to have many enemies. In 1679 he was appointed chaplain to Princess Mary, daughter of the Duke of York, she later became the wife of William Prince of Orange. Mary disliked his plain admonitions and had him dismissed. Ken was finally the Bishop of Bath and Wells, but was imprisoned in the Tower of London for three years by King James for his refusal to subscribe to the Declaration of Indulgence. Upon his release from prison he retired from public life, spending his closing years with his close friend Lord Weymouth. He devoted himself to the writing of hymns which were published in four volumes in 1721 following his death.

Thomas Ken will always be remembered for his immortal words in the form of doxology: "Praise God from Whom all blessings flow", which, doubtless, have been sung by more people than the words of any other writer.

PRAISE GOD, FROM WHOM ALL BLESSINGS FLOW

Hymn 359   Tune: *Old 100th*

Praise God, from whom all blessings flow;
Praise Him, all creatures here below;
Praise Him above, ye heavenly host:
Praise Father, Son, and Holy Ghost.

THOMAS KEN

JOHN KENT

Kent, John (Bideford, Devonshire, England, Dec. 1766—Plymouth, Nov. 15, 1843).

John Kent was born into a poor family, and so had little opportunity to obtain an education. The circumstances of his conversion are unknown, but he became a Christian while he was very young. At the age of fourteen he showed a remarkable ability to write poetry. In 1803 a small volume was published containing a collection of his original hymns. Hymnologists quickly saw the value and beauty of his work, and John Kent was given a foremost place among writers. Later in life he lost his eyesight, this he bore with great patience, and finished his course in triumph. His last words were, "I am accepted in the Well-Beloved".

Three of John Kent's hymns are included in the Believers Hymn Book. Unlike many of the writers of hymns, who had education, wealth, and honourable positions, John Kent was poor, uneducated and lastly blind. However it is often God's way to use the weak things of the world to confound the mighty, that glory might be brought to His great Name (1 Cor. 1:27).

O BLESSED GOD HOW KIND

Hymn 181 Tune: *Lenox*

O Blessed God! how kind
 Are all Thy ways to me,
Whose dark benighted mind
 Was enmity with Thee.
Yet now, subdued by sovereign grace,
My spirit longs for Thine embrace.

Preserved by Jesus, when
 My feet made haste to hell!
And there should I have gone,
 But Thou dost all things well:
Thy love was great, Thy mercy free,
Which from the pit delivered me.

Sovereign grace! o'er sin abounding 249
Hark! how the blood-bought hosts above 338

JOHN KENT

HOWARD KINGSBURY

Kingsbury, Howard (c.1850).
Very little information can be obtained concerning this writer. The name Howard Kingsbury has always been associated with the well known hymn "God is love". It is evident from the beautiful language of the hymn that the writer appreciated God's wondrous love in giving His Son to the death of the Cross (John 3:16).

GOD IS LOVE

Hymn 39   Tune: *Better World*

Come, let us all unite to sing,
    God is love.
Let heaven and earth their praises bring;
    God is love.
Let every soul from sin awake,
Each in his heart sweet music make,
And sing with us, for Jesus' sake,
    God is love.

HOWARD KINGSBURY

SAMUEL CHRISTIAN GOTTFRIED KUSTER

Kuster, Samuel Christian Gottfried (Havelberg, Germany, Aug. 18, 1762—Aberswalde, Germany, Aug. 22, 1838).

Samuel Christian Gottfried Kuster graduated with a D.D. degree from the University of Berlin. He began his ministry as pastor of the Lutheran church in Werder, Berlin. His preaching was marked by faithfulness to the Word of God. As a hymn writer Kuster was well known for the beauty and spiritual depth of his compositions. He also wrote a valuable volume on the origin of some early hymns.

His best known hymn "Lord Jesus, Friend unfailing" was translated into English by Hannah Burlingham and was first published in the *British Herald* July 1865.

This hymn has been a comfort and guide to many Christians and is included in the Believers Hymn Book.

LORD JESUS FRIEND UNFAILING

Hymn 131   Tune: *Tyrolese*

Lord Jesus, Friend unfailing!
 How dear Thou art to me!
Are cares or fears assailing?
 I find my strength in Thee:
Why should my feet grow weary
 Of this my pilgrim way?
Rough though the path and dreary,
 It ends in perfect day.

O worldly pomp and glory,
 Your charms are spread in vain;
I've heard a sweeter story,
 I've found a truer gain.
Where Christ a place prepareth,
 There is my loved abode,
There shall I gaze on Jesus,
 There shall I dwell with God.

SAMUEL CHRISTIAN GOTTFRIED KUSTER

MARY ARTEMISIA LATHBURY

Lathbury, Mary Artemisia (Manchester, New York, U.S.A. Aug. 10, 1841—East Orange, N. Jersey, Oct. 20, 1913).

Mary Lathbury was the daughter of a Methodist minister. She was a professional artist, and a gifted poet, who wrote prose and verse for children. Much of her poetry first appeared in a youth publication for the Methodist Sunday School Union, of which she was general editor.

"Break Thou the Bread of Life" was written as a hymn to be sung before Bible Study in connection with Chautauqua Conference Centre in New York State. This beautiful hymn was based on the feeding of the five thousand by Christ, beside the Sea of Galilee, the idea being that souls might feed upon Christ, so that lives may be faithful in testimony.

BREAK THOU THE BREAD OF LIFE

Hymn 373   Tune: *Lathbury*

Break Thou the bread of life,
　Dear Lord, to me,
As Thou didst break the loaves
　Beside the sea;
Beyond the sacred page
　I seek Thee, Lord;
My spirit pants for Thee,
　O living Word.

Open Thy word of truth
　That I may see
Thy message written clear
　And plain for me;
Then, in sweet fellowship,
　Walking with Thee,
Thine image on my life
　Engraved will be.

Bless Thou the truth, dear Lord,
　To me, to me,
As thou didst bless the bread
　By Galilee;
Then shall all bondage cease,
　All fetters fall;
And I shall find my peace,
　My all in all.

MARY ARTEMISIA LATHBURY

JOHANN CASPAR LAVATER

Lavater, Johann Caspar (Zurich, Switzerland, Nov. 15, 1741, Zurich, Jan 2, 1801).

Johann Caspar Lavater was the son of a physician in Zurich. He studied at the Academic Gymnasium in Zurich, and although ordained in 1762 he did not become pastor of the Orphanage Church in Zurich until 1775. In 1776 he was appointed pastor of St. Peters in Zurich.

During the Revolutionary period he was outspoken in the pulpit and as a result was imprisoned by the French for a short time in 1779. Later he was shot by a French grenadier, who had just thanked him for his charity. Lavater never fully recovered from his wound.

The devotional writings of Johann Lavater were eagerly read and admired all over Europe, but soon forgotten. Only some of his many hymns were ever translated into English. His finest hymn; "O Jesus Christus, wachs in mir" was translated "O Jesus Christ, grow Thou in me" and is preserved for the use of those who sing from the Believers Hymn Book. The hymn is based on John 3:30 "He must increase, but I must decrease".

O JESUS CHRIST, GROW THOU IN ME

Hymn 424   Tune: *Caithness*

O Jesus Christ, grow Thou in me,
  And all things else recede;
My heart be daily nearer Thee,
  From sin be daily freed.

More of Thy glory let me see,
  Thou holy, wise and true;
I would Thy living image be,
  In joy and sorrow too.

Make this poor self grow less and less,
  Be Thou my life and aim;
O make me daily, through Thy grace,
  More meet to bear Thy Name.

JOHANN CASPAR LAVATER

JANE ELIZA LEESON

Leeson, Jane Eliza (Nottingham, England, 1807—1882).

Little is known of Jane E. Leeson's personal history, although she wrote many hymns, was the author of children's books, and translated many well known hymns from the Latin.

"Have ye counted the cost, ye warriors of the Cross?" was first published in a hymnal, *Songs of Christian Chivalry* in 1848. The hymn had ten verses but these have been abbreviated in the Believers Hymn Book.

HAVE YOU COUNTED THE COST?

Hymn 66   Tune: *Resolution*

Have ye counted the cost,
Have ye counted the cost,
Ye warriors of the Cross?
Are ye fixed in heart for your Master's sake,
To suffer all earthly loss?
Can ye bear the scoff of the worldly-wise,
As ye pass by pleasure's bower,
To watch with your Lord on the mountain-top,
Through the dreary midnight hour?

JANE ELIZA LEESON

WILLIAM FREEMAN LLOYD

Lloyd, William Freeman (Alley, Gloucestershire, England, Dec. 22, 1791—Stanley Hall, England, April 22, 1853).

William Lloyd was saved early in life. He was greatly interested in Sunday School work. In 1810 he was appointed secretary of the Sunday School Union. He commenced a magazine for Sunday School teachers, and for years edited *Children's Companion*. His beautiful hymn "Our times are in Thy hand" first appeared in the hymnal of G.V. Wigram *Hymns for the Poor of the Flock*. Lloyd passed home to be with Christ from Stanley Hall the home of his brother Dr. Samuel Lloyd.

OUR TIMES ARE IN THY HAND

Hymn 222   Tune: *Swabia*

Our times are in Thy hand;
  Father, we wish them there!
Our life, our souls, our all we leave
  Entirely to Thy care.

Our times are in Thy hand,
  Jesus the crucified!
The hand our many sins have pierced
  Is now our guard and guide.

Our times are in Thy hand;
  We'll always trust in Thee,
Till we have left this weary land,
  And all Thy glory see.

WILLIAM FREEMAN LLOYD

PHILIP DODDRIDGE AND JOHN LOGAN

Logan, John (Fala, Scotland, 1748—London, Dec. 28, 1788).
There is much controversy surrounding the hymn writing of John Logan. Experts in the realm of hymnology say that he revised eight of the Paraphrases. It is not clear whether he or Michael Bruce wrote some of the hymns attributed to him. "O God of Bethel by whose hand" was written by Philip Doddridge and revised by John Logan. It was the favourite of David Livingstone and was sung at his funeral in Westminster Abbey, in 1874.
John Logan ministered in South Leith for twelve years.
After being the author of a drama, which was withdrawn from the stage after its first showing in Edinburgh, he moved to London, where he died an embittered man.

O GOD OF BETHEL

Hymn 422   Tune: *Salzburg*

O God of Bethel! by whose hand
 Thy people still are fed;
Who through this weary pilgrimage
 Hast all our fathers led.

O spread Thy covering wings around
 Till all our wanderings cease,
And at our Father's loved abode
 Our souls arrive in peace.

Such blessings from Thy gracious hand
 Our humble prayers implore;
And Thou shalt be our chosen God,
 And portion evermore.

PHILIP DODDRIDGE and JOHN LOGAN

ROBERT LOWRY

Lowry, Robert (Philadelphia, U.S.A. March 12, 1826—Plainfield, N. Jersey, Nov. 25, 1899).

Robert Lowry was educated at Bucknell University graduating with honours in 1854. He was the Baptist pastor in Plainfield the greater part of his life. He had a great ability in composing suitable hymn tunes, which he did for many well known writers. Robert Lowry was also a very gifted hymn writer. He wrote such hymns as "Shall we gather at the river", "What can wash away my stain", "My home is in heaven", "Weeping will not save thee" etc. His greatest hymn celebrates the glorious Resurrection of the Lord Jesus "Low in the grave He lay". It was written in 1874 and published in *Brightest and Best*, a magazine with a large circulation in that day. This beautiful hymn has been included in the Believers Hymn Book, and is still as popular as when first sung in Plainfield over 100 years ago.

LOW IN THE GRAVE HE LAY

Hymn 344   Tune: *Christ Arose* by Robert Lowry

    Low in the grave He lay,
      Jesus, my Saviour,
    Waiting the coming day,
      Jesus, my Lord.

Up from the grave He arose
With a mighty triumph o'er His foes;
He arose a victor from the dark domain,
And He lives for ever with His saints to reign;
    He arose! He arose!
    Hallelujah! Christ arose!

    Death cannot keep his prey,
      Jesus, my Saviour,
    He tore the bars away,
      Jesus, my Lord.

ROBERT LOWRY

HENRY FRANCIS LYTE

Lyte, Henry Francis (Kelso, Scotland, June 1, 1793—Nice, France, Nov. 20, 1847).

Henry Francis Lyte was educated at Portora Royal School in Enniskillen, Northern Ireland, and Trinity College, Dublin. He intended to be a physician but instead became a minister of the Church of England, although not a born-again Christian. Three years later another clergy man who was dying in agony of soul sent for Lyte to visit him. Lyte sat at the bedside of the dying man and read Paul's epistles to him. Through this unique occasion both men trusted Christ alone for salvation.

In 1813 Lyte was appointed curate in Brixham, England—a seafaring town. His ministry was greatly blessed of God among the townsfolk and a large Sunday School of over 800 children was gathered, in which he took a special interest.

One writer says that Henry Lyte's life was filled with disappointment and affliction. He wrote many beautiful hymns, but the last one he wrote has been used in many stirring and emotional moments in history: "Abide with me" was written shortly before he died. It is based upon the words of the two disciples at the village of Emmaus, when they said to the Lord "Abide with us for it is toward evening and the day is far spent" (Luke 24:29).

MY REST IS IN HEAVEN

Hymn 160   Tune: *Maryport*

My rest is in heaven, my rest is not here,
Then why should I murmur when trials are
    near?
Be hushed my sad spirit, the worst that can
    come
But shortens the journey and hastens me
    home.

The winds of affliction around me may blow,
And dash my lone barque as I'm sailing below;
I smile at the storm as I lean on His breast,
And soon I shall land in the haven of rest.

With Christ in my heart, and His Word in my
    hand,
I travel in haste through an enemy's land;
The road may be rough, but it cannot be long,
So I journey on singing the conqueror's song.

Praise, my soul, the King of heaven.................... 438

HENRY FRANCIS LYTE

MARTIN MADAN

Madan, Martin (Hertingford, Bury, England, 1726—Epsom, England, 1790).

Martin Madan was the son of Colonel Martin Madan, and a cousin of William Cowper, the well known hymn-writer. He studied law at Christ Church Oxford, and was called to the Bar in 1748. With other lawyers he went to hear and ridicule the preaching of John Wesley, but instead was awakened to see his sinful condition, and through the preaching of the gospel was saved on that evening.

Martin Madan is not known to have written any hymns himself, but he had great ability in adapting and revising the work of others. It is through his compositive work that many of the great hymns of the eighteenth century are still popular today.

He compositely completed John Bakewell's great hymn "Hail, Thou once despisèd Jesus" and "Lo, He comes with clouds descending" with Charles Wesley and John Cennick.

Hail, Thou once despisèd Jesus 61
Lo, He comes with clouds descending 408

These hymns were compositely written by John Bakewell, Charles Wesley, John Cennick and Martin Madan.

MARTIN MADAN

JOHN
MARRIOTT

Marriott, John (Lutterworth, England, 1780—Exeter, 1825).
John Marriott was well educated graduating from Oxford with a master's degree. He became tutor in the Palace of Dalkeith to Lord George Scott.
Marriott was an evangelical in his belief, and was also a man of great personal charm. Sir Walter Scott dedicated his ballad "Marmion" in his honour.
As a hymn-writer Marriott ranks among the foremost in his generation. Modesty would not allow him to publish any of his hymns during his lifetime. After his death they appeared in print. The most sublime and valuable of all his spiritual songs "Thou whose almighty word, chaos and darkness heard" has survived, and is included in the Believers Hymn Book.

THOU WHOSE ALMIGHTY WORD

Hymn 457   Tune: *Moscow*

Thou whose almighty word
Chaos and darkness heard,
    And took their flight,
Hear us, we humbly pray,
And, where the gospel day
Sheds not its glorious ray,
    Let there be light.

Thou who didst come to bring,
On Thy redeeming wing,
    Healing and sight,
Health to the sick in mind,
Sight to the inly blind,
O now to all mankind
    Let there be light.

Blessèd and holy Three,
Glorious Trinity,
    Wisdom, Love, Might,
Boundless as ocean's tide
Rolling in fullest pride,
Through the world, far and wide,
    Let there be light.

JOHN MARRIOTT

JOHN MASON

Mason, John (Northants, England, 1646—Water, Stratford, 1694).

The known facts concerning John Mason are few. He was the son of a non-conformist minister, and the grandfather of John Mason the author of *A Treatise on Self-Knowledge*. He was educated at Cambridge University. In 1673 he became Rector of Water-Stratford. Here he composed *The Songs of Praise*. His hymns were spiritual and were much eulogised by Isaac Watts. It is believed that the hymns of Mason greatly influenced the writings of Watts, and the Wesleys.

A volume of John Mason's original works of 1686 are in the British Museum in London.

John Mason is best remembered by his greatest hymn "I've found the precious Christ of God".

I'VE FOUND THE PRECIOUS CHRIST OF GOD

Hymn 107   Tune: *Belgrave*

I've found the precious Christ of God,
  My heart doth sing for joy;
And sing I must, for Christ I have,
  A precious Christ have I.

Christ is my Shepherd and my Friend,
  My Saviour whom I love,
My Head, my Hope, my Counsellor,
  My Advocate above.

Christ Jesus is the heaven of heaven;
  My Christ what shall I call?
Christ is the First, Christ is the Last,
  And Christ is all in all.

JOHN MASON

GEORGE MATHESON

Matheson, George (Glasgow, Scotland, 27th March, 1842— North Berwick, Scotland, 28th August, 1906).

George Matheson gradually lost his vision until by the age of eighteen he was almost blind. Nevertheless he was a brilliant student at Glasgow University. He became minister of St. Bernards, Edinburgh in 1886 but resigned in 1899 because of poor health. Matheson wrote a number of books of theology, and a volume of sacred songs. He was one of the outstanding preachers of his day. On one occasion he was summoned to preach to Queen Victoria at Balmoral Castle. It is recorded the Queen was inspired by his message.

"O Love that wilt not let me go" is the only hymn that he wrote that is remembered today. It is said that he was in love but the girl gave him up when she realised he was going blind. Over twenty years later when his sister was married the affair in his life was recalled and gave rise to the writing of the beautiful hymn, in which he extolled the unchanging love of Christ. He himself stated: "The writing of the hymn was the quickest work I ever accomplished in my life". He had no natural gift of composing yet the whole hymn was completed in five minutes. It seems as if he received special inspiration in the writing of this spiritual song.

O LOVE THAT WILT NOT LET ME GO

Hymn 428   Tune: *St. Margaret*

O Love that wilt not let me go,
I rest my weary soul in Thee;
I give Thee back the life I owe,
That in Thine ocean depths its flow
  May richer, fuller be.

O Joy that seekest me through pain,
I cannot close my heart to Thee;
I trace the rainbow through the rain,
And feel the promise is not vain
  That morn shall tearless be.

O cross that liftest up my head,
I dare not ask to fly from thee,
I lay in dust life's glory dead,
And from the ground there blossoms red
  Life that shall endless be.

GEORGE MATHESON

MARY ELIZABETH MAXWELL

Maxwell, Mary E (Richmond, England, Oct. 4, 1837—Richmond, Feb. 4, 1915).

This hymn has been associated with the Keswick Convention in the North of England and has been ascribed to Mary E. Maxwell. She was Mary E. Braddon, and was educated at home by private tutors and became a prolific author. She married John Maxwell in 1874, and wrote the beautiful hymn "Channels only, blessèd Master" for use at Keswick. The tune was written by Ada Rose Gibbs and was first published with the words in *Twenty-Four Gems of Sacred Song* in 1900. The hymn is included in the Believers Hymn Book and is often sung in preparation for ministry from the Scriptures.

CHANNELS ONLY

Hymn 393   Tune: *Channels Only*

How I praise Thee, precious Saviour!
That Thy love laid hold of me;
Thou hast saved and cleansed and filled me,
That I might Thy channel be.

Channels only, blessèd Master,
But with all Thy wondrous power
Flowing through us, Thou canst use us
Every day and every hour.

MARY ELIZABETH MAXWELL

SAMUEL MEDLEY

Medley, Samuel (Chesnut, England, June 23, 1738—Liverpool, July 17, 1799).

Samuel Medley served in the Royal Navy and was severely wounded off Port Lagos in 1759. His father, who was a believer, was a personal friend of Isaac Newton. In 1762 Medley came to know his sins forgiven through reading a sermon of Isaac Watts on Isaiah 42:6,7. He wrote the beautiful words of "Awake, my soul, in joyful lays" to commemorate this happy occasion of his conversion to God. He became a faithful preacher of the gospel spending most of his life as pastor in Byron St. Baptist Church in Liverpool. Many souls were saved through his ministry. Samuel Medley was a prolific hymn writer. In all he wrote 230 hymns. These were marked by devotion to the Lord and the spirit of thanksgiving and worship to the Father. Five of his sacred melodies are included in the Believers Hymn Book. These are sung frequently by believers in every place where praise is offered to God.

AWAKE MY SOUL IN JOYFUL LAYS

Hymn 10   Tune: *Gardenstown*

Awake, my soul, in joyful lays,
And sing thy great Redeemer's praise;
He justly claims a song from thee;
His loving-kindness—O how free!

He saw me ruined in the fall,
Yet loved me notwithstanding all;
He saved me from my lost estate;
His loving-kindness—O how great!

When trouble, like a gloomy cloud,
Has gathered thick and thundered loud,
He near my soul has ever stood;
His loving-kindness—O how good!

Come, let us sing the matchless worth 40
Now, in a song of grateful praise 169
On Christ salvation rests secure 212
The Saviour lives, no more to die 280

SAMUEL MEDLEY

ALBERT MIDLANE

Midlane, Albert (Isle of Wight, Jan. 23, 1825—Isle of Wight, Feb. 28, 1909).

Albert Midlane was brought up in a home where his father was not interested in spiritual matters, but his mother was saved and was used of the Lord in teaching him the Scriptures and had the joy finally of seeing him trust Christ as his Saviour. He was associated with brethren and had the privilege of hearing the ministry of J.N. Darby and William Kelly. Later he was in fellowship in the assembly in the Isle of Wight, where he continued stedfastly all his life. He owned an ironmongery business for over fifty years.

In 1859 he contributed a poem to C.H. Macintosh for his magazine *Good news for the Young*. This poem, which became a hymn: "There's a Friend for little children, above the bright blue sky" was to find its way into over 200 hymn books. It is sung in China, Japan, India, Europe, America, Africa, Australia, and in most unlikely parts of the world, as well as being translated into more than a hundred languages, and will likely be sung "while the earth remaineth". The author lived to see the jubilee of his best-known hymn, and had the great pleasure of hearing three thousand children sing it in St. Pauls Cathedral. Lord Tennyson, the poet laureate, said of the hymn that it was the sweetest ever heard. Albert Midlane wrote many other beautiful hymns. God had given him a wonderful ability in the realm of hymnody. Unlike many authors he derived no monetary benefit, or took out "copyright" for any of his hymns. He has left a priceless legacy to the Church and the world.

LORD JESUS THINE

Hymn 138   Tune: *Patience*

    Lord Jesus, Thine;
      No more this heart of mine
Shall seek its joy apart from Thee;
The world is crucified to me,
      And I am Thine.

    Thine, Thine alone,
      My joy, my hope, my crown;
Now earthly things may fade and die,
They charm my soul no more, for I
      Am Thine alone.

    Till Thou shalt come
      And bear me to Thy home,
For ever freed from earthly care,
Eternally Thy love to share:
      Lord Jesus, come!

Revive Thy work, O Lord 242
Without a cloud between 351

ALBERT MIDLANE

E.M. MILN

Miln, E.M.
Of this hymn writer we have no available information. Her touching hymn appears in *Hymns of Light and Love* also. The value she placed upon the Cross of Christ and His glorious Person is evident in the hymn.

THE CROSS! THE CROSS!

Hymn 264

The Cross! the Cross!
The Christian's only glory;
I see the standard rise:
    March on, march on,
The Cross of Christ before thee;
That Cross all hell defies.

The Cross! the Cross!
Redemption's standard raising;
I see the banner wave:
    Sing on, sing on,
Salvation's Captain praising;
'Tis Christ alone can save.

E.M. MILN

A.B. MACKAY

Mackay, A.B.
This beautiful hymn of pilgrimage shows the spiritual pathway of the Lord's People from the Cross to the Crown. Of the writer we have been unable to obtain any information at this time.

WE'RE A PILGRIM BAND
IN A STRANGER LAND

Hymn 314

We're a pilgrim band in a stranger land,
  Who are marching from Calvary,
Where the wondrous Cross, with its gain and
    loss,
  Is the sum of our history:
There we lost our stand in a death-doomed
    land,
  As children of wrath by the fall;
There we gained a place as heirs of grace,
  At the feast in the heavenly hall.

A.B. MACKAY

THEODORE MONOD

Monod, Theodore (Paris, Nov. 6, 1836—Lyons, France, 1921).

Theodore Monod was an outstanding French Christian. He was saved in boyhood. He was educated at Western Theological Seminary, Allegheny, Pa. U.S.A. Upon graduating Dr. Monod was pastor in the French Reformed Church of Paris, France. He was a faithful preacher of the gospel and saw many saved. Later in 1880 he moved to Lyons and there with a company of fellow-believers assembled according to the principles of the New Testament, having left the various churches in the area. Many of them were Roman Catholics. John Nelson Darby visited them and the company was established, great numbers were added, and other companies were formed. Monod wrote one beautiful hymn which is in the Believers Hymn Book. It evidences the humility of the writer and his aspirations after the knowledge of Christ.

O THE BITTER SHAME AND SORROW

Hymn 430   Tune: *St. Jude*

O the bitter shame and sorrow!
  That a time could ever be
When I let the Saviour's pity
Plead in vain; and proudly answered,
  All of self, and none of Thee!

Yet He found me: I beheld Him
  Bleeding on the accursèd tree:
Heard Him pray: Forgive them, Father!
And my wistful heart said faintly,
  Some of self, and some of Thee!

Day by day His tender mercy,
  Healing, helping, full and free:
Sweet and strong, and ah! so patient,
Brought me lower, while I whispered,
  Less of self, and more of Thee!

Higher than the highest heaven,
  Deeper than the deepest sea,
Lord, Thy love at last hath conquered;
Grant me now my supplication—
  None of self, and all of Thee!

THEODORE MONOD

JOHN SAMUEL BEWLEY MONSELL

Monsell, John Samuel Bewley (Londonderry, Northern Ireland, Mar. 2, 1811—Guildford, England, April 9, 1875).

John Monsell was the son of an archdeacon of Londonderry, and brother of the first Lord Emily. He was educated at Trinity College Dublin. On graduation he entered the ministry of the Church of England and finally became rector of Guildford Cathedral in Surrey.

Monsell published 11 volumes of poetry including over 300 hymns. He was a strong advocate that congregational singing should be more "fervent and joyous".

John Monsell was accidentally killed by falling masonry whilst he was watching operations in connection with the renovation of the Guildford church. Two of his hymns are in the Believers Hymn Book.

TO THEE, O GRACIOUS SAVIOUR!

Hymn 301   Tune: *Munich*

To Thee, O gracious Saviour!
  My spirit turns for rest,
My peace is in Thy favour,
  My pillow on Thy breast:
Though all the world deceive me,
  I know that I am Thine,
And Thou wilt never leave me,
  O blessèd Saviour mine!

Alas, that I should ever
  Have failed in love to Thee,
The only One who never
  Forgot or slighted me!
O for a heart to love Thee
  More truly as I ought,
And nothing place above Thee
  In deed, or word, or thought!

Fight the good fight with all thy might 381

JOHN SAMUEL BEWLEY MONSELL

JAMES MONTGOMERY

Montgomery, James (Irvine, Scotland, Nov. 4, 1771—Sheffield, England, April 30, 1854).

James Montgomery was the son of the only Moravian minister in Scotland. He was educated at Fulneck Seminary near Leeds, but made very little progress at school, and was dismissed because of his pre-occupation with writing poetry. Years later he became editor and owner of a newspaper in Sheffield, where he was outspoken in his writings in opposition to slavery. He was assured of salvation when forty three years of age. At that time he visited the Moravian village of Gracehill, Northern Ireland. In that peaceful village he was inspired to write some of his greatest hymns. In all Montgomery penned over 400 hymns which appeared in two hymn books *Songs of Zion* and *The Christian Psalmist*.

Dr. John Julian, the eminent hymnologist, writes of Montgomery: "The secrets of his power as a writer of hymns were manifold. His poetic genius was of a high order. His knowledge of the Scriptures was most extensive. His devotional spirit was of the highest type. With the faith of a strong man he united the beauty and simplicity of a child."

ACCORDING TO THY GRACIOUS WORD

Hymn 5   Tune: *Martyrdom*

According to Thy gracious Word,
  In meek humility,
This would I do, O Christ my Lord,
  I would remember Thee.

Gethsemane can I forget?
  Or there Thy conflict see,
Thine agony and blood-like sweat,
  And not remember Thee?

When to the Cross I turn mine eyes,
  And rest on Calvary,
O Lamb of God, my sacrifice,
  I must remember Thee.

For ever with the Lord 48
Prayer is the soul's sincere desire 234
The Lord Himself shall come 272
Hail to the Lord's Anointed 389

JAMES MONTGOMERY

THOMAS MOORE

Moore, Thomas (Dublin, Ireland, May 28, 1779—Devizes, England, Feb. 25, 1852).

Thomas Moore studied law at Middle Temple, London. He was appointed admiralty registrar in Bermuda. The position was not to his pleasure so he appointed a deputy and returned to England. He was financially ruined by the deputy's embezzlement, and was exiled to Europe until the money was repaid. Upon settlement Moore returned to England. He wrote a number of hymns, 32 of which were published in *Sacred Songs 1816*. "Sound the high praises of Jesus, the King" is one of his best hymns. Thomas Moore, while of evangelical belief, remained a member of the Roman Catholic Church.

SOUND THE HIGH PRAISES OF JESUS

Hymn 247　　Tune: *Victory*

Sound the high praises of Jesus, the King!
He came and He conquered—His victory sing;
Sing, for the power of the tyrant is broken;
The triumph complete over death and the grave.
Vain is their boasting; Jehovah hath spoken,
And Jesus proclaimed Himself mighty to save,
Sound the high praises of Jesus, the King!
He came and He conquered—His victory sing.

THOMAS MOORE

JOHN MORISON

Morison, John (Aberdeen, Scotland, 1798).

John Morison was a minister in Scotland. He translated the hymn: " 'Twas on that night when doomed to know" for use as a communion hymn. The Latin original was the work of Dr. Andrews Elinger, a medical professor of Jena in 1552.

'TWAS ON THAT NIGHT

Hymn 459   Tune: *Rockingham*

'Twas on that night, when doomed to know
The eager rage of every foe,
That night in which He was betrayed,
The Saviour of the world took bread.

And after thanks and glory given
To Him that rules in earth and heaven,
That symbol of His flesh He broke,
And thus to all His followers spoke.

My body broken thus I give
For you, for all; take, eat, and live:
And oft the sacred rite renew
That brings My wondrous love to view.

JOHN MORISON

WILLIAM MORSHEAD

Morshead, Wm. (Bath, England—c.1833).
Very little information is obtainable about William Morshead further than he was associated with brethren from the beginning of the recovery of the Truth, and was intimately acquainted with J.N. Darby, John Bellet, and Dr. Cronin.
His hymn 341 is an epitome of Divine Truth:

JESUS, THE CHRIST! ETERNAL WORD!

Hymn 341

Jesus, the Christ! Eternal Word!
Of all creation Sovereign Lord!
On Thee alone by faith we rest,
And lean our weakness on Thy breast.

Thy blood hath washed us from our sin;
Thy Spirit sanctifies within;
And Thou for us in all our need
At God's right hand dost ever plead.

WILLIAM MORSHEAD

HANDLEY CARR GLYN MOULE

Moule, Handley Carr Glyn (Fordington, England, Dec. 23, 1841—Liverpool, 1920).

Handley C.G. Moule was educated at home by private tutor, and at Trinity College, Cambridge. He was a brilliant student and graduated with first class honours in Classical Literature and Theology. He became Principal of Ridley College Cambridge in 1880. For a number of years he was the Select Preacher at Cambridge University. Principal Moule was also chaplain to the Bishop of Liverpool, where he moved to live in 1887.

He was a Bible expositor, writing commentaries on the Epistles to the Romans, Ephesians and Philippians, which are still used as text-books. He also contributed to Smith's Bible Handbook.

As a hymn writer he was considered in the foremost rank, on account of the depth of teaching and the beauty of language in his hymns.

"My glorious Victor, Prince divine" in the Believers Hymn Book is an example of his ability.

MY GLORIOUS VICTOR

Hymn 419   Tune: *Staincliffe*

My glorious Victor, Prince divine,
Clasp these surrendered hands in Thine;
At length my will is all Thine own,
Glad vassal of a Saviour's throne.

My Master, lead me to Thy door;
Pierce this now willing ear once more:
Thy bonds are freedom; let me stay
With Thee to toil, endure, obey.

Yes, ear and hand, and thought and will,
Use all in Thy dear slavery still;
Self's weary liberties I cast
Beneath Thy feet; there keep them fast.

HANDLEY CARR GLYNN MOULE

EDWARD MOTE

Mote, Edward (London, Jan. 21, 1797—Southwark, Nov. 13, 1874).

Edward Mote came to know Christ as his Saviour while yet young. He worked as a carpenter during the day, and as an evangelist in the evening. He was asked to become pastor at Horsham Baptist Church which he accepted in 1852, and continued there all his life. Many souls were saved and large numbers of children gathered in the Sunday School.

Edward Mote wrote over 100 hymns, but his first hymn has out-lived them all.

"My hope is built on nothing less" was written as he was going to work, before he became a preacher. He completed the beautiful song in one day. Today it is the only hymn in common use which he wrote.

THE SOLID ROCK

Hymn 158

My hope is built on nothing less
Than Jesus' blood and righteousness;
I dare not trust the sweetest frame,
But wholly lean on Jesus' Name.
    On Christ, the solid Rock, I stand;
    All other ground is sinking sand.

When darkness seems to veil His face,
I rest on His unchanging grace;
In every high and stormy gale
My anchor holds within the veil.
    On Christ, the solid Rock, I stand;
    All other ground is sinking sand.

When darkness seems to veil His face,
I rest on His unchanging grace;
In every high and stormy gale
My anchor holds within the veil.
    On Christ, the solid Rock, I stand;
    All other ground is sinking sand.

EDWARD MOTE

BERTHA MULLEN

Mullen, Bertha (1959).

Bertha Mullen has written one of the finest consecration hymns "Break every barrier down" which ranks alongside Francis R. Havergal's hymn "Take my life and let it be".

Concerning the writer we have no available information at present. The beautiful suitable tune was composed by William Eddy Vine.

BREAK EVERY BARRIER DOWN

Hymn 371   Tune: *Moncton*

Break every barrier down,
Thou Lamb of Calvary;
Show me the awfulness of sin,
  The thing which grieveth Thee:
Purge Thou my soul from dross,
Cleanse me from every sin,
Wash me in Thine atoning blood,
  And make me pure within.

Break every barrier down
And reign triumphant, Lord;
May every breathing of my heart
  With Thine be in accord:
Grant me to enter in
The secret place with Thee,
To walk with Thee, as Enoch walked,
  Into eternity.

BERTHA MULLEN

ROBERT A.S. MACALISTER

Macalister, Robert Alexander Stewart. A.R.C.O., F.S.A., Litt.D.D. (Dublin, Ireland, 1870—Dublin, 1950).

Robert A.S. Macalister was educated at Rathmines School, Dublin, and a German Private School, and at Cambridge University. He had many degrees and was a specialist in the field of archaeology. In 1923-4 he led a group in connection with the Palestine Exploration Society, who discovered part of the walls and fortifications of the most ancient Jerusalem. He also discovered the Jebusites fortress, Millo, which retained its independence until King David stormed it and set up Zion. This had been one of the missing links in the historical reconstruction of Jerusalem. The discovery settled the site of the city of David on the eastern hill.

Macalister was evangelical in his faith, and was marked by a humble spirit. He was a fine musician and was organist at Adelaide St. Presbyterian Church in Dublin for many years. He composed music for many sacred songs and hymns. As a translator of hymns from Latin and German into English he did considerable research. His beautiful hymn included in the Believers Hymn Book is full of teaching and devotion. Macalister went home to be with Christ at the age of eighty.

LOOK UPON US BLESSED LORD

Hymn 411   Tune: *Liebster Jesu*

Look upon us, blessèd Lord,
Take our wandering thoughts and guide us;
We have come to hear Thy word,
With Thy teaching now provide us,
That, from earth's distractions turning,
We Thy message may be learning.

Brightness of the Father's face,
Light of light, from God proceeding,
Make us ready in this place;
Ear and heart await Thy leading:
In our study, prayers and praising,
May our souls find their upraising.

Written compositely by
TOBIAS CLAUSNITZER and ROBERT A.S. MACALISTER

ROBERT MURRAY McCHEYNE

McCheyne, Robert Murray (Edinburgh, May 11, 1813—Dundee, March 25, 1843).
Robert Murray McCheyne was a genius from childhood. He was able to sing and recite fluently, and knew the letters of the Greek alphabet at the age of four. He was educated at Edinburgh University and became a minister in Dundee. His fame as a preacher spread far and near and many came to hear his faithful messages. He wore himself out by his strenuous labours and the intensity of spirit with which he preached the Word. After two years his health gave way and he was unable to continue preaching. At that time he was sent to Palestine as a member of a committee of inquiry into the possibility of evangelisation among Jews. Andrew Bonar accompanied him and they wrote a most interesting account of their visit to the land. McCheyne died at the early age of 29 years, leaving behind the influence of his godly life which was felt in the city of Dundee and far beyond for many years.
Robert Murray McCheyne was also a hymn-writer of note. His hymns were published under the title *Songs of Zion*. Two of his best compositions are preserved in the Believers Hymn Book.

I ONCE WAS A STRANGER

Hymn 96   Tune: *Tsidkenu*

I once was a stranger to grace and to God;
I knew not my danger, I felt not my load;
Though friends spoke in rapture of Christ on the tree,
Jehovah Tsidkenu was nothing to me.

Like tears from the daughters of Zion that roll,
I wept when the waters went over His soul;
Yet thought not that my sins had nailed to the tree
Jehovah Tsidkenu—'twas nothing to me.

My terrors all vanished before the sweet Name;
My guilty fears banished, with boldness I came
To drink at the fountain, life-giving and free;
Jehovah Tsidkenu is all things to me.

When this passing world is done 356

ROBERT MURRAY McCHEYNE

JAMES McGRANAHAN

McGranahan, James (Adamsville, PA. July 4, 1840—Kinsman, Ohio, July 7, 1907).

James McGranahan trusted Christ as his Saviour when he was fourteen years of age. He had an inborn love of music, and loved to sing of Christ all the days of his life. He and Philip Bliss were great friends, and the companionship produced glory to God in their devoted service to the Lord. On the homecall of Bliss, the evangelistic ministry was continued by McGranahan, who associated himself with Major Whittle in missions both in America and Great Britain. This co-operation was continued for many years, and large numbers were brought to Christ through their faithful presentation of the Gospel. As an editor of hymnals and a compiler of music McGranahan was associated with Ira. D. Sankey, George Stebbins and G.F. Root.

Two of his best known hymns are often sung by Christians and are included in the Believers Hymn Book.

VERILY, VERILY, I SAY UNTO YOU

Hymn 209 Tune by James McGranahan

O what a Saviour, that He died for me!
From condemnation He hath made me free;
"He that believeth on the Son," saith He,
 "Hath everlasting life."

"Verily, verily, I say unto you;"
"Verily, verily," message ever new!
"He that believeth on the Son," 'tis true
 "Hath everlasting life."

Though all unworthy, yet I will not doubt;
For him that cometh He will not cast out;
"He that believeth," O the good news shout!
 "Hath everlasting life."

Far, far away, in heathen darkness dwelling 379

JAMES McGRANAHAN

DR. WILLIAM PATON MACKAY

Mackay, William Paton (Montrose, Scotland, May 13, 1839—Oban, Scotland, Aug. 22, 1885).

William Paton Mackay graduated from Edinburgh University with an M.D. He gave up his medical practice when thirty years old, having heard the call to preach the gospel, which had won his heart. He spent most of his life ministering the Word and preaching the Gospel in the city of Hull, England, and the surrounding villages and towns. Many were saved through his faithful efforts. He took a leading role in the visit of Moody and Sankey to England in 1873-74. D.L. Moody acknowledged the great blessing he had derived from the teaching ministry of Dr. Mackay. Dr. Mackay wrote a useful book entitled *Grace and Truth*. He also penned a number of very interesting hymns, but the three in the Believers Hymn Book are considered his best.

Dr. Mackay met with a serious accident, as he was going on board a ferry when on holiday at Oban, Scotland, and died the following day. He left behind a fragrant testimony, and hymns that exalt the Person and Work of the Lord Jesus Christ.

WORTHY, WORTHY IS THE LAMB

Hymn 328   Tune: *Warwick Lane*

Worthy, worthy is the Lamb!
Worthy, worthy is the Lamb!
Worthy, worthy is the Lamb!
That was slain.

Praise Him, hallelujah!
Bless Him, hallelujah!
Praise Him, hallelujah!
Praise the Lamb!

We shall ever reign with Thee
We shall ever reign with Thee
We shall ever reign with Thee
Lamb of God.

The Lord is risen: now death's dark judgment flood 277
We praise Thy great love 313

Dr. WILLIAM PATON MACKAY

JOACHIM NEANDER

Neander, Joachim (Bremen, Germany, 1650—Bremen, 1680).

Joachim Neander has been linked with Paulus Gerhardt as the two greatest hymn-writers of Europe. Neander was educated at the Padagonium in Bremen. During student days he joined with the rebellious element so prevalent in those days. He was later converted listening to the powerful preaching of Theodore Under-Eyck, who was mightily used of God in the salvation of souls. For the next ten years Neander lived for Christ and wrote many beautiful hymns. Being also a gifted musician he composed music for over sixty of his hymns. Joachim was the first important German hymn-writer of the German Reformed Church.

Many of his hymns were written, like David, in a cave overlooking the beautiful Neanderthal valley.

Neander died at the early age of 30, leaving a legacy to the Church in spiritual songs.

PRAISE TO THE LORD

Hymn 439 Tune: *Lobe Den Herren*

Praise to the Lord, the Almighty, the King
 of creation;
O my soul, praise Him, for He is thy health
 and salvation;
  All ye who hear,
  Brethren and sisters draw near,
  Praise Him in glad adoration.

Praise to the Lord, O let all that is in me adore
 Him;
All that hath life and breath come now with
 praises before Him;
  Let the Amen
  Sound from His people again:
  Gladly for aye we adore Him.

JOACHIM NEANDER

DR. DAVID NELSON

Nelson, David (Tennessee, U.S.A., Sept. 24, 1793—Quincy, Ill. Oct. 17, 1844).

Dr. David Nelson was a surgeon in the U.S. Army in the war of 1812. He was an infidel during his service but after the war turned to God for salvation and became a devoted Christian. On returning to his plantation in Missouri he was determined to free all his slaves. This brought great anger from his neighbours; they forced him to flee his home, and hunted him through woods and swamps for three days and three nights. He finally reached the Mississippi river. On the other side was the free state of Illinois. He hid in a clump of bushes on the riverside waiting for darkness. As he lay there in danger of capture, he looked across the swiftly flowing river to the land of freedom on the other side, and the lines of his beautiful hymn began to form in his mind. He carefully wrote these down; thus "My days are gliding swiftly by" was born.

Later that night he escaped his enemies, when a small canoe rescued him and brought him across to the Illinois shore at Quincy.

Dr. Nelson preached the gospel and lived Christ in Quincy till his homecall in 1844.

MY DAYS ARE GLIDING SWIFTLY BY

Hymn 151 Tune: *Meikle Holm*

My days are gliding swiftly by,
 And I, a pilgrim stranger,
Would not detain them as they fly,
 These hours of toil and danger.

For O we stand on Jordan's strand,
 Our friends are passing over,
And just before, the shining shore
 We may almost discover.

Should coming days be cold and dark,
 We need not cease our singing;
That perfect rest nought can molest,
 Where golden harps are ringing.

Dr. DAVID NELSON

JOHN NEWTON

Newton, John (London, England, July 24, 1725—London England, Dec. 21, 1807).

In recent years John Newton has become world famous through the revival of his hymn "Amazing grace".

John Newton went to sea with his father who was a captain in the Merchant Navy. He finally became a captain himself and sailed the slave ships, during which time he lived a life of sin and drunkenness. One night in a terrible storm at sea when men were swept overboard and the ship seemed doomed, Newton turned to God in repentance and cried upon God for mercy. The words of Scripture, taught by his godly mother, came into his mind, and he was led to trust the One whose Name became altogether lovely to him forever. John Newton became a changed man, a great preacher and a writer of many beautiful hymns. He worked with William Cowper in producing the *Olney Hymn Book*.

One of his best loved hymns is "How sweet the Name of Jesus sounds".

In the church of St. Marys, Woolnoth, London, is the epitaph written by himself:

"John Newton, once an infidel, a servant of slaves in Africa, was, by the rich mercy of God and our Saviour Jesus Christ, pardoned, and appointed to preach the faith he had once laboured to destroy."

Ten of his hymns are included in the Believers Hymn Book, and are in constant use among the saints.

THE NAME ABOVE ALL OTHERS

Hymn 79   Tune: *St. Peter*

How sweet the Name of Jesus sounds
  In a believer's ear!
It soothes his sorrows, heals his wounds,
  And drives away his fear.

Dear Name! the Rock on which we build;
  Our shield and hiding-place;
Our never-failing treasury, filled
  With boundless stores of grace.

Behold the throne of grace............................ 18
Begone unbelief! my Saviour is near 27
Great Shepherd of Thy chosen flock 59
Let us love and sing and wonder 124
Let us rejoice in Christ 125
May the grace of Christ our Saviour................... 145
Sweeter sounds than music knows 257
Poor, weak, and worthless though I am 349
Come, my soul, thy suit prepare 374

JOHN NEWTON

CAROLINE MARIA NOEL

Noel, Caroline Maria (London, England, April 10, 1817—London, Dec. 7, 1877).

Caroline Maria Noel was the daughter of the Hon. Gerrard Thomas Noel, who was also a well known hymn writer. She was also a niece of the Hon. Baptist Noel, a noted evangelist. She became a Christian in early life and wrote her first hymns at seventeen years of age. For over twenty years her pen was silent. As the result of suffering through ill health she wrote again. During the last twenty-five years of her life as an invalid she wrote many hymns which convey comfort to others, the comfort with which she herself was comforted of God.

She published *The Name of Jesus, and other verses for the sick and lonely* in 1861 and a second volume titled *The Precious Name of Jesus* was published the year after her homecall. Her greatest hymn "In the Name of Jesus every knee shall bow" included in the Believers Hymn Book is a favourite in the assemblies of the saints.

IN THE NAME OF JESUS
EVERY KNEE SHALL BOW

Hymn 397   Tune: *Evelyns*

In the name of Jesus every knee shall bow,
Every tongue confess Him King of glory
   now;
'Tis the Father's pleasure we should call Him
   Lord,
Who from the beginning was the mighty Word.

Humbled for a season to receive a name
From the lips of sinners unto whom He came;
Faithfully He bore it spotless to the last,
Brought it back victorious when from death
   He passed.

Brethren, this Lord Jesus shall return again,
With His Father's glory, with His angel train;
For all wreaths of empire meet upon His brow,
And our hearts confess Him King of glory
   now.

CAROLINE MARIA NOEL

THOMAS OLIVERS

Olivers, Thomas (Tregynon, Wales, 1725—London, 1799).

Thomas Oliver was orphaned at the age of four, and raised on a farm by distant relatives. He led a confused and restless life until he heard George Whitefield preach the gospel from the text "Is not this a brand plucked out of the burning?" He became a Christian. His life was changed, he paid his debts and joined the Wesleys as an itinerant preacher. For the next 22 years he preached the gospel, travelling on horseback throughout England and Wales. He finally disagreed with the Wesleys and retired to London. Charles Wesley said of him "He is a good man, though a rough stick of wood". The one hymn which he wrote is a masterpiece. God truly used the weak things of earth to confound the mighty when he chose Thomas Olivers, who had no education or noble background, to write one of the most majestic hymns of praise ever penned. This excellent hymn is found in the Believers Hymn Book.

THE GOD OF ABRAHAM PRAISE

Hymn 273   Tune: *Leona*

The God of Abraham praise,
Who reigns enthroned above,
Ancient of everlasting days,
And God of love.
Jehovah, great I AM!
By earth and heaven confessed,
I bow and bless the sacred Name,
For ever blessed.

The God of Abraham praise,
Whose all-sufficient grace
Shall guide me all my pilgrim days,
In all my ways.
He calls a worm His friend,
He calls Himself my God;
And He shall save me to the end,
Through Jesus' blood.

THOMAS OLIVERS

CATESBY PAGET

Paget, Catesby.

Concerning Catesby Paget no information is presently available. The only hymn ascribed to this writer expresses the joy of heart of a saint who found peace with God through the precious blood of His Son.

The words of this song seem to be founded on another song yet to be sung in the land of Judah "Thou wilt keep him in perfect peace, whose mind is stayed on Thee, because He trusteth in Thee" (Isa. 26:1-4).

A MIND AT PERFECT PEACE WITH GOD

Hymn 3   Tune: *Richmond*

A mind at perfect peace with God,
  Oh! what a word is this!
A sinner reconciled through blood;
  This, this indeed is peace!

Why should I ever careful be,
  Since such a God is mine?
He watches o'er me night and day,
  And tells me "Mine is thine."

CATESBY PAGET

DR. RAY PALMER

Palmer, Ray (Rhode Island, U.S.A. Nov. 12, 1808—Newark, N.J. Mar. 29, 1887).

Ray Palmer is the foremost American hymn-writer, and deserves a place beside the most accomplished English-speaking writers. He wrote more hymns than any other American, some of unsurpassed beauty and tenderness. He was educated at Yale University, and became a minister of the Congregational Church. He served long terms in Maine and finally in Albany, New York. When he retired he made his home in Newark, where he led an active life in evangelism until he died in his eightieth year.

It is as a hymn-writer that Dr. Palmer is best known. He was a model writer of high standard. The poetic and hymnic elements were present in his work.

Two of his widely known hymns are "My faith looks up to Thee" and "Jesus, these eyes have never seen".

Dr. Ray Palmer was an accomplished translator from the Latin. His translation of Bernard's *"Jesu, Dulcedo cordium"* is one of the best renderings of "Jesus, Thou Joy of loving hearts" and is included in the Believers Hymn Book.

JESUS THOU JOY OF LOVING HEARTS

Hymn 404   Tune: *Hereford*

Jesus, Thou joy of loving hearts,
Thou fount of life, Thou light of men,
From the best bliss that earth imparts
We turn unfilled to Thee again.

Thy truth unchanged hath ever stood;
Thou savest those that on Thee call;
To them that seek Thee Thou art good;
To them that find Thee, all in all.

O Jesus ever with us stay,
Make all our moments calm and bright;
Chase the dark night of sin away;
Shed o'er the world Thy holy light.

Written by BERNARD OF CLAIRVAUX
Translated by Dr. RAY PALMER

EDWARD PERRONET

Perronet, Edward (Kent, England, 1726—Canterbury, 1792).
Edward Perronet was an eccentric preacher associated with the Wesleys and would have long since been forgotten but for his one great hymn which has been given a place in the four greatest Christian hymns. Those four hymns are printed in more collections, translated into more languages, and sung by more people than any others. They are "The Wondrous Cross" by Isaac Watts, "Rock of Ages" by Augustus Toplady, "Jesus, Lover of my soul" by Charles Wesley, and "Coronation" by Edward Perronet. The last verse of the hymn is said to have been added by John Rippon in 1787.

CORONATION

Hymn 361   Tune: *Miles Lane*

All hail the power of Jesus' name!
  Let angels prostrate fall;
Bring forth the royal diadem
  And crown Him Lord of all!

Sinners, whose love can ne'er forget
  The wormwood and the gall,
Go, spread your trophies at His feet,
  And crown Him Lord of all!

Let every kindred, every tribe,
  On this terrestrial ball,
To Him all majesty ascribe,
  And crown Him Lord of all!

EDWARD PERRONET

MARY PETERS

Peters, Mary (Mary Bowley) (Cirencester, England, April 17, 1813—Bristol, England, July 29, 1856).

Mary Bowley was a very spiritual woman, she was saved in childhood. She married John Peters when only 17 years old. John Peters died four years later. Following his death Mary Peters began to write hymns. In the next twelve years she wrote 58 beautiful hymns of tenderness and worship. These were published in 1847 as *Hymns to help the Communion of saints*. Twelve have been included in the Believers Hymn Book. They form a delightful outline of the glories of the Name and Person of our Lord Jesus Christ.

Mary Peters was called home at the early age of forty three. Her choice hymns are a treasured legacy of priceless worth and are specially appreciated and sung in the assemblies of the Lord's people.

O LORD, HOW MUCH THY NAME UNFOLDS

Hymn 201   Tune: *St. Agnes, Durham*

O Lord, how much Thy Name unfolds
  To every opened ear;
The pardoned sinner's memory holds
  None other half so dear.

The mention of Thy Name shall bow
  Our hearts to worship Thee;
The chiefest of ten thousand Thou!
  The chief of sinners we.

Around Thy table, holy Lord 4
Blessed Lord, our souls are longing 19
Lord Jesus, in Thy Name alone 135
O Blessed Lord, what hast Thou done 173
Of Thee, Lord, we would never tire 184
Praise ye the Lord again 236
Salvation to our God 246
The holiest now we enter 270
Through the love of God our Saviour 296
'Tis we, O Lord, whom Thou hast shown 300
Unworthy our thanksgiving 306

MARY PETERS

DR. SYLVANUS DRYDEN PHELPS

Phelps, Sylvanus Dryden (Suffield Conn. U.S.A. May 15, 1816—New Haven, Nov. 23, 1895).

Dr. S.D. Phelps was converted as a student at the Connecticut Literary Institution in Suffield. He became the minister in the First Baptist Church in New Haven and continued there for thirty years. He was a faithful preacher of the Gospel and was a man of humble spirit. He wrote one hymn of grateful devotion to Christ which was first published in *Pure Gold* 1871. The usual title of the beautiful hymn is "Something for Jesus". The meaning and sentiment of both words and music are not unlike Francis Havergal's "I gave My life for Thee".

Dr. Phelp's hymn has been given a rightful place in the Believers Hymn Book.

SOMETHING FOR THEE

Hymn 443   Tune: *Offering*

Saviour, Thy dying love
Thou gavest me,
Nor should I aught withhold,
   My Lord, from Thee;
In love my soul would bow,
My heart fulfil its vow,
Some offering bring Thee now,
   Something for Thee.

All that I am and have,
   Thy gifts so free;
In joy, in grief, through life,
   O Lord, for Thee!
And when Thy face I see
My ransomed soul shall be,
Through all eternity,
   Something for Thee.

Dr. SYLVANUS DRYDEN PHELPS

DR. ARTHUR TAPPAN PIERSON

Pierson, Arthur Tappan (New York, March 6, 1837—Philadelphia, 1911).

Dr. A.T. Pierson was educated at Hamilton College. He was a Presbyterian minister, first for a number of years in Detroit and lastly at Bethany Church in Philadelphia. He was a man of deep convictions relative to the great fundamentals of Scripture, and opposed the inroads of modernism in his day. He wrote a number of excellent books on such subjects as: *The Authority of the Bible, The Resurrection of Christ, The Second Advent.*

Dr. Pierson also was an excellent hymn writer, his best known being a gospel hymn entitled: "The Gospel of Thy Grace my stubborn heart has won." This is one of the few gospel hymns suitable for such a service, included in the Believers Hymn Book.

THE GOSPEL OF THY GRACE

Hymn 267　　　Tune: *Good News*

The Gospel of Thy Grace
My stubborn heart has won;
For God so loved the world,
　He gave His only Son,
　　That "Whosoever will believe,
　　Shall everlasting life receive!"
　　Shall everlasting life receive!

The serpent "lifted up"
　Could life and healing give,
So Jesus on the Cross
　Bids me to look and live.

Dr. ARTHUR TAPPAN PIERSON

JEAN SOPHIA PIGGOTT

Piggott, Jean Sophia (Co. Kildare, Ireland, 1845—Lucan, Ireland, 1882).

Very little information is available concerning Jean S. Piggott. She died at the early age of 37.

Her hymn shows her spiritual character and the peace she enjoyed in Christ.

James Mountain composed the tune and the hymn was first published in *Hymns of Consecration and Faith.*

JESUS, I AM RESTING

Hymn 400   Tune: *Tranquillity*

Jesus, I am resting, resting
  In the joy of what Thou art;
I am finding out the greatness
  Of Thy loving heart:
Thou hast bid me gaze upon Thee,
  And Thy beauty fills my soul,
For, by Thy transforming power,
  Thou hast made me whole.

  Jesus, I am resting, resting
    In the joy of what Thou art;
  I am finding out the greatness
    Of Thy loving heart.

JEAN SOPHIA PIGGOTT

JOHN PRICE

Price, John. (c.1805).
Information regarding John Price is not available.
Dr. John Julian gives a very brief notice. He states that the hymn "Higher than I" is ascribed to John Price by Daniel Sedgwick in 1805."
The beautiful words of this hymn have brought comfort to many tried saints and have given fresh courage to hide in that Rock, which is Christ.

HIGHER THAN I

Hymn 99   Tune: *Hiding in Thee*

In seasons of grief to my God I'll repair,
When my heart is o'erwhelmed with sorrow and care;
From the ends of the earth to Thee will I cry,
Lead me to the Rock that is higher than I.

   Higher than I, higher than I,
   Lead me to the Rock that is higher than I.

JOHN PRICE

EDWARD C. QUINE

Quine, Edward C. (Douglas, Isle of Man, 1857—Douglas, 1942).

Edward C. Quine was born in the Isle of Man of Methodist parentage. He became a Christian in his early life. Shortly afterwards he was led by the reading of the Scriptures to associate himself with the small assembly of believers gathered to the Lord's Name at Athol St. in Douglas. He remained with the assemblies for the fifty years of his Christian life. He was a true Pastor, Teacher and Evangelist, labouring in the Word, and in the spread of the Gospel in many parts of the British Isles, twenty five of those years in the Isle of Man.

One outstanding hymn came from his pen which is treasured among the Lord's people everywhere, and has a rightful place in the Believers Hymn Book: "Glory to Thee, Thou Son of God Most High."

Edward C. Quine's great hymn is a legacy which he has left to the Church.

GLORY TO THEE; THOU SON OF GOD MOST HIGH

Hymn 386   Tune: *Sandon*

Glory to Thee; Thou Son of God most High,
    All praise to Thee!
Glory to Thee, enthroned above the sky,
    Who died for me;
High on Thy throne, Thine ear, Lord Jesus, bend
As grateful hearts now to Thyself ascend.

Thorns wreathed Thy brow when hanging on the tree,
    Man's cruelty!
Why lavish love like this, O Lord, on me?
    Thou lovest me!
Would that my soul could understand its length,
Its breadth, depth, height, and everlasting strength!

Like shoreless seas, Thy love can know no bound;
    Thou lovest me!
Deep, vast, immense, unfathomed, Lord— profound,
    Lord, I love Thee!
And when above, my crown is at Thy feet,
I'll praise Thee still for Calvary's mercy seat.

EDWARD C. QUINE

BENJAMIN MANSELL RAMSEY

Ramsey, Benjamin Mansell (Richmond, Surrey, England, 1849—Chichester, Sussex, Aug. 31, 1923).

Very little is known of this writer as all records were destroyed by a fire.

Benjamin M. Ramsey was well known as a teacher in the Bournemouth area. He was a writer of carols and hymns and a composer of pianoforte pieces.

One of his greatest hymns based upon Psalm 27:11 is: "Teach me Thy way, O Lord" and is included in the Believers Hymn Book. The suitable tune "Camacha" was written by the author himself.

TEACH ME THY WAY, O LORD

Hymn 447

Teach me Thy way, O Lord,
Teach me Thy way;
Thy gracious aid afford,
Teach me Thy way:
Help me to walk aright,
More by faith, less by sight;
Lead me with heavenly light,
Teach me Thy way.

BENJAMIN MANSELL RAMSEY

GEORGE RAWSON

Rawson, George (Leeds, England, June 5, 1807—Clifton, England, March 25, 1889).

George Rawson practised as a lawyer in Leeds for many years. He was a devoted Christian with a fervent interest in the composition of hymns based on the Scriptures.

He wrote over fifty hymns and was extremely modest about his own hymn-writing, signing them A *Leeds Lawyer*.

Two outstanding hymns are in use today: "Cast Thy burden on the Lord" from Psalm 55:22, and "By Christ redeemed, by Christ restored" based on 1 Cor. 11:26.

The latter is a beautiful "remembrance hymn" which is often sung at the Lord's Supper. The important phrase "Until He Come" is used as a refrain at the end of each stanza, and emphasises the prospect of the Coming Again of the Lord Jesus.

BY CHRIST REDEEMED, IN CHRIST RESTORED

Hymn 372   Tune: *Memoria*

By Christ redeemed, in Christ restored,
We keep the memory adored,
And show the death of our dear Lord
    Until He come.

His body, broken in our stead,
Is seen in this memorial bread,
And so our feeble love is fed
    Until He come.

The drops of His dread agony,
His life-blood shed for us, we see;
The wine shall tell the mystery
    Until He come.

O blessèd hope! with this elate,
Let not our hearts be desolate,
But, strong in faith, in patience wait
    Until He come.

GEORGE RAWSON

WILLIAM REID

Reid, William (Forfar, Scotland, 1822—Edinburgh, Aug 8, 1881).

William Reid was saved while a boy at school. He entered the ministry of the Presbyterian Church at Carlisle, in the North of England. He was a faithful gospel preacher and an able minister of God's Word. His clear outline of apostolic teaching and practise led to a serious division in his congregation. William Reid found it impossible to continue in what he believed to be an unscriptural position, so resigned, and a large number also left the church at the same time. These commenced to gather according to the Word of God to the Name of the Lord alone, and to carry out the principles practised by the infant Church; thus one of the earliest New Testament assemblies was planted in Carlisle.

William Reid edited the magazine *British Herald* which was a gospel monthly with a wide circulation. He also wrote a book entitled *The Blood of Jesus* which has been greatly used in the salvation of souls. The Hymn Book *Songs of Redemption* which he edited contained many of his hymns, two of which are in the Believers Hymn Book. William Reid was a man who left behind a fragrant testimony of godly living and deep humility.

MID THE SPLENDOURS OF THE GLORY

Hymn 150   Tune: *Lewes*

Mid the splendours of the glory,
  Which we hope ere long to share,
Christ, our Head, and we, His members,
  Shall appear divinely fair;
    O how glorious!
  When we meet Him in the air!

Bright the prospect soon that greets us
  Of that longed-for nuptial day,
When our heavenly Bridegroom meets us
  On His kingly, conquering way;
    In the glory,
  Bride and Bridegroom reign for aye!

Ours are peace and joy divine........................224

WILLIAM REID

THOMAS H. REYNOLDS

Reynolds, Thomas H. (Burford, England, March 1830—Oxford, Feb. 1930).

Thomas H. Reynolds was saved through the faithful preaching of the gospel by an evangelist called George Page, who was mightily used of God around Oxfordshire in 1840-50. The converts were gathered together in assembly capacity, and taught the ways of the Lord. Such a company was found in an upper room, over a bookstore in Burford, where a few believers gathered to "break bread" and study the Scriptures.

Reynolds soon came into fellowship and continued in the enjoyment of the truth for 85 years. He became a diligent student of the Word of God, and was proficient in his knowledge of Hebrew and Greek. His ministry was Christ-exalting in character.

Thomas Reynolds is best remembered by his beautiful hymn of communion, so suitable for singing at the Lord's Supper, which he himself ever appreciated.

T.H. Reynolds died in his one hundredth year, finishing his course with joy.

JESUS LORD WE COME TOGETHER

Hymn 401   Tune: *Firenze*

Jesus, Lord, we come together
   In the bonds of Thine own love;
Thou hast drawn our footsteps hither
   Its deep meaning now to prove.

Here together we recall Thee,
   In Thy presence break the bread;
Never more can grief befall Thee,
   Thou art risen from the dead.

But Thy love remains, that entered
   Into death to make us Thine;
In that death all love was centred;
   Thankful now we drink the wine.

Sweet it is to sit before Thee,
   Sweet to hear Thy blessèd voice,
Sweet to worship and adore Thee,
   For our hearts in Thee rejoice.

THOMAS H. REYNOLDS

ROBERT ROBINSON

Robinson, Robert (Cambridge, England, Sept. 27, 1735—London, June 9, 1790).
Robert Robinson was a poor boy left an orphan at an early age. He came to Christ through the faithful preaching of George Whitefield, and dedicated himself to the service of the Lord. He preached with various groups, but ever seemed unstable in his doctrine and ways. The reference to his "wandering heart" in his hymn gives an insight into his character. He finally drifted away from the joy of God. The story is told that while travelling in a stage-coach a lady sitting opposite asked him had he ever heard the hymn "Come, Thou fount of every blessing, Tune my heart to sing Thy praise", as it had given her comfort in times of sorrow. He replied "Madam, I am the poor unhappy man who composed that hymn many years ago and I would give a thousand worlds, if I had them, to enjoy the feelings I had then."

COME THOU FOUNT OF EVERY BLESSING

Hymn 43   Tune: *Sharon*

Come, Thou Fount of every blessing,
  Tune my heart to sing Thy grace;
Streams of mercy, never ceasing,
  Call for songs of loudest praise.

Jesus sought me when a stranger,
  Wandering from the fold of God;
He, to save my soul from danger,
  Interposed His precious blood.

O to grace how great a debtor
  Daily I'm constrained to be!
Let that grace, Lord, like a fetter,
  Bind my wandering heart to Thee.

ROBERT ROBINSON

DR. HENRI L. ROSSIER

Rossier, Dr. Henri L. (Vevey, Switzerland, Jan 25, 1835—Vevey, Mar. 20, 1928).
Dr. Henri L. Rossier was born into a family that was among the first in Switzerland to gather unto the Name of the Lord Jesus alone. Rossier studied medicine at Zurich and Wurzburg and upon gaining his M.D. returned to his native Vevey, and practised medicine for over fifty years. As time went on he increasingly devoted himself to ministry and Bible Conferences among brethren in different parts of Europe. He translated the Synopsis by J.N. Darby into French from English. He also was editor of a monthly magazine for the edification of the believers throughout the French-speaking world, Dr. Rossier also wrote commentaries on many parts of the Scriptures. He was a prolific hymn-writer. His twenty eight hymns appearing in the *Hymnes Et Cantiques* the hymn book used in French-speaking assemblies, are full of devotion and thanksgiving to the Father for His Son. One of these delightful hymns has been included in the Believers Hymn Book. After a long and useful life of service for the Lord, Dr. Rossier was called home at the advanced age of 93 years.

LORD E'EN TO DEATH THY LOVE COULD GO

Hymn 409   Tune: *St. Marguerite*

Lord, e'en to death Thy love could go,
  A death of shame and loss,
To vanquish for us every foe,
  And break the strong man's force.

O what a load was Thine to bear,
  Alone in that dark hour,
Our sins in all their terror there,
  God's wrath and Satan's power.

The storm that bowed Thy blessèd head
  Is hushed for ever now,
And rest divine is ours instead,
  Whilst glory crowns Thy brow.

Within the Father's house on high
  We soon shall sing Thy praise;
But here, where Thou didst bleed and die,
  We learn that song to raise.

Dr. HENRI L. ROSSIER

FRANCIS ROUS

Rous, Francis (Halton, Cornwall, England, 1579—Acton, Jan. 7, 1659).

Francis Rous revised the original paraphrase of King David's beautiful Shepherd Psalm 23, composed by William Whittingham, and together they have given hymnology one of the most beautiful spiritual renderings of the Psalm. This paraphrase represents the most familiar and best loved of all the Psalms of the Scottish Church. Wherever sung to the beautiful tune "Crimond" it awakens a thrill of memory and devotion.

It was chosen by Queen Elizabeth II to be sung on the wonderful day of her Coronation. Spurgeon once said, "Psalm 23 is like a handful of snow upon a fevered brow". It truly is the "Pearl of all the Psalms".

THE LORD'S MY SHEPHERD

Hymn 454   Tune: *Crimond*

The Lord's my Shepherd, I'll not want:
  He makes me down to lie
In pastures green; He leadeth me
  The quiet waters by.

My soul He doth restore again;
  And me to walk doth make
Within the paths of righteousness,
  E'en for His own name's sake.

Goodness and mercy all my life
  Shall surely follow me;
And in God's house for evermore
  My dwelling-place shall be.

Ye gates lift up your heads on high 463

Compositely written by William Whittingham
  and Francis Rous 454
Compositely written by Francis Rous
  and William Barton 463

FRANCIS ROUS

DOUGLAS RUSSELL

Russell, Douglas (Ayr, Scotland, 1842—Weston-Super-Mare, Nov. 14, 1933).

Douglas Russell was saved listening to the preaching of E. Payson Hammond, an American evangelist who visited Scotland. Russell was then 19 years of age. He was baptised and received into assembly fellowship in Edinburgh. A few years later he was called to the full-time service of the Lord and went forth trusting God to supply his need. He preached with good results in Canada, Australia, and New Zealand as well as the British Isles.

Douglas Russell was a great personal friend of Ira D. Sankey. Like Sankey he was a prolific composer, hymn-writer and singer. He visited Ira Sankey, in New York, shortly before his death. He sang one of his new pieces to Sankey "I love to make the story known". Sankey remarked "It is those who preach the gospel who are best equipped to write gospel songs."

Douglas Russell wrote 150 beautiful hymns, published in a volume entitled *Songs of Salvation and Glory*. Many of these are included in *Hymns of Light and Love*, but only one in the Believers Hymn Book. He was called home in his ninety second year.

GATHERED LORD AROUND THY TABLE

Hymn 383 Tune: *Bullinger*

Gathered, Lord, around Thy table,
  Now we seek Thy face;
Let us know Thy presence with us,
  Lord of Grace.

Love divine first drew us to Thee
  In our sin and need;
For our sin, in deep compassion,
  Thou didst bleed.

Gratefully we Thee remember
  As we break the bread,
Symbol of Thy body broken
  In our stead.

Backward look we, drawn to Calvary,
  Musing while we sing;
Forward haste we to Thy coming,
  Lord and King.

DOUGLAS RUSSELL

ARCHIBALD J. RUTHERFORD

Rutherford, Archibald J. (Scotland, c.1775).
Very little information is available concerning Archibald J. Rutherford, except that he wrote eight hymns found in an old Scottish hymn book. His two hymns in the Believers Hymn Book leave no doubt as to the foundation of his faith, his love to the Person of Christ, and his hope of heaven through the Saviour's redeeming blood.

GLORY UNTO JESUS BE!

Hymn 54   Tune: *Harts*

Glory unto Jesus be!
Thou from wrath didst set us free;
All our guilt on Thee was laid,
Thou our ransom-price hast paid.

All should sing Thy work and worth,
All above, and all on earth;
We shall sing around the throne,
"Thou art worthy, Thou alone."

The countless multitude on high 265

ARCHIBALD J. RUTHERFORD

JOHN RYLAND

Ryland, John (London, England, Jan. 29, 1753— London, Jan. 25, 1825).

John Ryland had the great blessing of a godly mother, who, like Eunice, the mother of Timothy, taught him the Scriptures which were able to make him wise unto salvation.

John Ryland was possessed of outstanding mental ability. At nine years of age he had mastered the Greek text and was able to read all the Greek New Testament. He became a prolific hymn-writer, authoring over 100 hymns. One of his best known and best loved compositions is in the Believers Hymn Book. He received an honorary doctorate from Brown University, Rhode Island, U.S.A. for his contribution to hymnology.

In 1794 he was appointed President of the Baptist College in Bristol, England, where he continued until his death in 1825. His last words were "and there shall be no more pain".

O LORD, I WOULD DELIGHT IN THEE

Hymn 200   Tune: *Beatitudo*

O Lord, I would delight in Thee,
　And on Thy care depend;
To Thee in every trouble flee,
　My best, my only Friend.

When all created streams are dried,
　Thy fulness is the same;
May I with this be satisfied,
　And glory in Thy Name.

O Lord, I cast my care on Thee;
　I triumph and adore;
Henceforth my great concern shall be
　To love and praise Thee more.

JOHN RYLAND

JOSEPH MEDICOTT SCRIVEN

Scriven, Joseph Medicott (Seapatrick, Banbridge, Nth. Ireland, Sept. 10, 1819—Bewdley, Port Hope, Ontario, Canada, Aug. 10, 1886).

Joseph Scriven's father was an officer in the Royal Marines. The family was wealthy and owned a large estate in Nth. Ireland. Scriven was educated at Trinity College, Dublin. While in Dublin he heard the gospel preached in Merrion Hall, and after a time of conviction was led to trust the Saviour. He associated himself with the brethren at Merrion Hall. His father was very opposed to this association, so two years after his graduation Joseph Scriven was forced to leave home and take up his teaching profession in Canada. He taught in Woodstock and Brantford and then was employed by Lieutenant Pengelly, a retired naval officer, as tutor to his family, near Port Hope.

Jospeh Scriven had two great tragedies in his life. On the eve of his wedding-day, his bride-to-be was drowned. This took place in Ireland before he emigrated. Once again he was engaged to be married, only to lose his second fiancee through a serious illness.

In spite of these losses, loneliness, poverty, and poor health, Scriven spent his life helping others and preaching the Word among the assemblies in Ontario. The words of his beautiful hymn were written for his mother in a time of deep distress. The manuscript is still a treasured possession of the Pengelly's family. Ira D. Sankey included the hymn as Number One in his *Gospel Hymn Book*, and it has been sung in congregations of Christians throughout the English-speaking world.

An unlettered person can understand the hymn, the humblest believer can take its comfort to heart, and all can prove that Jesus is indeed an all-sufficient Friend.

The people of Port Hope and district erected a monument to his memory near Rice Lake, as an appreciation of his untiring labours to help the poor and needy.

WHAT A FRIEND WE HAVE IN JESUS

Hymn 317 Tune: *Converse*

What a Friend we have in Jesus,
  All our sins and griefs to bear!
What a privilege to carry
  Everything to God in prayer!
O what peace we often forfeit,
  O what needless pain we bear!
All because we do not carry
  Everything to God in prayer.

Have we trials and temptations?
  Is there trouble anywhere?
We should never be discouraged:
  Take it to the Lord in prayer!
Can we find a friend so faithful,
  Who will all our sorrows share?
Jesus knows our every weakness:
  Take it to the Lord in prayer!

JOSEPH MEDICOTT SCRIVEN

MARY SHEKLETON

Shekleton, Mary (Dublin, Ireland, 1827—Dublin, 1883).
   Mary Shekleton was a semi-invalid the greater part of her life, like many other women hymn-writers.
   Francis Ridley Havergal said of her, "Mary Shekleton was one of the many sofa workers who do what they can and beyond that are content to wait."
   Mary Shekleton formed "The Invalid Prayer Union" which made a bond with invalid Christians in her native Ireland and throughout the world. A memorial of her life is entitled:—
   "Chosen, Chastened, Crowned".
   The most beautiful hymn from her pen is perhaps "It passeth knowledge that dear love of Thine". Probably she based her hymn upon the words of Paul. "And to know the love of Christ which passeth knowledge" (Eph. 3:19).

IT PASSETH KNOWLEDGE, THAT DEAR LOVE OF THINE

Hymn 101

It passeth knowledge, that dear love of Thine,
Lord Jesus, Saviour; yet this soul of mine
Would of Thy love, in all its breadth and length,
Its height and depth, its everlasting strength
                Know more and more.

It passeth telling, that dear love of Thine,
Lord Jesus, Saviour; yet these lips of mine
Would fain proclaim to sinners, far and near,
A love which can remove all guilt and fear,
                And love beget.

MARY SHEKLETON

SIR WALTER SHIRLEY

Shirley, Sir Walter (Galway, Ireland, 1725—Dublin, April 7, 1786).

Sir Walter Shirley was the grandson of the first Earl Ferrars and cousin of the Countess of Huntingdon, whose name was closely associated with the spiritual revival in the British Isles over two hundred years ago. After experiencing the great spiritual change of conversion Shirley entered the ministry of the Church of England. He was Rector of Loughgree, Galway, Ireland for many years. He was a close friend of George Whitefield and the Wesleys. His brother, the Earl of Ferrars, an ungodly man, murdered one of his faithful servants in a fit of rage, and was executed for the crime. Sir Walter, after the long disgrace of the trial, and final verdict, found great consolation in his consideration of the Cross.

In his saddest hours he wrote the beautiful hymn, by which his name is remembered: "Sweet the moments rich in blessing, which before the Cross we spend".

SWEET THE MOMENTS RICH IN BLESSING

Hymn 258   Tune: *Sharon*

Sweet the moments, rich in blessing,
 Which before the Cross we spend,
Life, and health, and peace possessing
 From the sinner's dying Friend.

Here we rest, in wonder viewing
 All our sins on Jesus laid,
And a full redemption flowing
 From the sacrifice He made.

May we still, the Cross discerning,
 There for peace and comfort go;
There new wonders daily learning,
 All the depths of mercy know.

Sir WALTER SHIRLEY

WILLIAM G. SLOAN

Sloan, William G. (Dalry, Scotland, 1835—Thorshaven, Faeroe Islands, 1914).

William G. Sloan was called of God to carry the Gospel to the Faeroe Islands in 1860. He went forth from his home assembly, Roman Rd., Motherwell, commended to the grace of God to carry out this task. Sloan sailed in a small fishing vessel from Papa Stour in the Shetlands to Thorshaven in the Faeroes. There he settled and laboured in the Gospel for 13 years without visible results. Finally God visited and gave times of great blessing through His servant, and the first Gospel Hall was erected in Thorshaven. Later many more were saved and assemblies increased in the islands until, today, ten per cent of the population gather in the Name of the Lord Jesus.

As a hymn-writer William Sloan gave the Faeroese Christians some beautiful hymns, one of which is in the Believers Hymn Book. This hymn is an epitome of his own experiences of God's faithfulness in his years of service in the Faeroe Islands.

PRAISE THE LORD, AND LEAVE TOMORROW

Hymn 229   Tune: *Corinth*

Praise the Lord, and leave to-morrow
In thy loving Father's hands;
Burden not thyself with sorrow,
   For secure the promise stands.
      He is faithful!
   Leave thy troubles in His hands.

Work to-day, and leave to-morrow,
All around there's urgent need;
All around there's sin and sorrow
   Broadcast, daily sow thy seed.
      God is faithful!
   He shall bless thy work indeed

WILLIAM G. SLOAN

JAMES GRINDLEY SMALL

Small, James Grindley (Edinburgh, 1817—Renfrew, Feb. 11, 1888).

James Grindley Small was educated at Edinburgh University. In 1847 he became minister of a Free Church near Melrose, Scotland. He wrote several poetical works including *Hymns for youth-ful voices*, and *Psalms and Sacred Songs*.

His best known hymn is "I've found a Friend, O such a Friend." Ira D. Sankey called this hymn one of his favourites and frequently sang it during Moody's great revival meetings.

The beautiful hymn has been often used in bringing souls to know the Friend of sinners.

I'VE FOUND A FRIEND

Hymn 103

I've found a friend; O such a Friend!
    He loved me ere I knew Him;
He drew me with the cords of love,
    And thus He bound me to Him.
And round my heart still closely twine
    Those ties which nought can sever,
For I am Christ's, and He is mine,
    For ever and for ever.

I've found a Friend; O such a Friend!
    He bled, He died to save me;
And not alone the gift of life,
    But His own self He gave me.
Nought that I have, mine own I'll call,
    I'll hold it for the Giver:
My heart, my strength, my life, my all,
    Are His, and His for ever.

JAMES GRINDLEY SMALL

JOSEPH DENHAM SMITH

Smith, Joseph Denham (Romsey, Hants, England, July 1816—Dublin, March 15, 1889).

Joseph Denham Smith first preached at the age of sixteen. He trained for the Congregational ministry in Dublin and was ordained a clergyman in 1840. He became dissatisfied with that position and resigned to be associated with brethren gathered to the Name of the Lord at Merrion Hall, Dublin. As an evangelist he preached throughout Ireland, and saw many souls saved. His health was never good and in 1886 he contracted an incurable disease. J.D. Smith preached his last message in Merrion Hall on July 26, 1887. Those present were deeply impressed with the character of the Word ministered concerning the Blessed Hope of the any-moment return of the Lord for His people. Joseph Denham Smith was one of the foremost hymn-writers of his day. Five of his hymns are in the Believers Hymn Book. His best known composition is "Rise, my soul, behold 'tis Jesus".

GOD'S ALMIGHTY ARMS ARE ROUND ME

Hymn 57   Tune: *Welsh Melody*

God's almighty arms are round me,
  Peace, peace, is mine!
Judgment scenes need not confound me,
  Peace, peace, is mine!
Jesus came Himself and sought me;
Sold to death, He found and bought me;
Then my blessèd freedom taught me,
  Peace, peace, is mine!

Welcome! every rising sunlight,
  Peace, peace, is mine!
Nearer home each rolling midnight,
  Peace, peace, is mine!
Death and hell cannot appal me,
Safe in Christ whate'er befall me,
Calmly wait I, till He call me,
  Peace, peace, is mine!

Just as Thou art, how wondrous fair................... 118
My God, I have found the thrice blessed ground 157
Rise, my soul, behold 'tis Jesus 238
Rise up and hasten! 241

JOSEPH DENHAM SMITH

WALTER CHALMERS SMITH

Smith, Walter Chalmers (Aberdeen, Dec. 5, 1824—Kinbuch, Sept. 20, 1908).

Walter Smith was educated at the University of Aberdeen. He was a minister of the Free Church of Scotland in Edinburgh, and became the Moderator of the Free Church in 1893.

Dr. Smith was an evangelical. He was a hymn-writer of note. His hymns were published under the title *Hymns of Christ and Christian Life*. One of these: "Immortal, Invisible, God only Wise" is a majestic hymn of worship, couched in the most exquisite language.

The hymn is based on the great words on Paul in 1 Tim. 1:17.

IMMORTAL, INVISIBLE, GOD ONLY WISE

Hymn 396   Tune: *St. Denio*

Immortal, invisible, God only wise,
In light inaccessible hid from our eyes,
Most blessèd, most glorious, the Ancient of
  Days,
Almighty, victorious, Thy great name we
  praise.

Great Father of glory, pure Father of light,
Thine angels adore Thee, all veiling their sight;
All laud we would render: O help us to see
'Tis only the splendour of light hideth Thee.

WALTER CHALMERS SMITH

HORATIO GATES SPAFFORD

Spafford, Horatio Gates (New York, U.S.A. Oct. 20, 1818—Jerusalem, Oct. 16, 1888).

Horatio Gates Spafford was a successful lawyer who practised in Chicago. He was professor of Medical jurisprudence to Chicago Medical College.

Spafford had a great interest in the archaeology of the Bible and made a number of visits to the Holy Land. He had large investments in real estate, but all his holdings were wiped out in the great Chicago fire. He also suffered the loss of his four daughters, who were drowned at sea, when the vessel on which the girls and their mother were travelling to Europe, *Ville du Havre*, was struck by the *Lochearn*, an English ship. The *Villa du Havre* sank in fifteen minutes. Spafford's wife was saved and sent a cable to her husband with two words "saved alone". Later, on his way across the Atlantic to meet his wife, Spafford wrote his well known hymn, near to the place where his daughters drowned.

Philip Bliss composed the tune for the hymn and titled it *Villa du Havre*. Horatio Gates Spafford and his wife formed the American Colony in Jerusalem, spending the remaining years of life in the Holy Land, where they engaged in evangelism among Jewish people.

WHEN PEACE LIKE A RIVER

Hymn 324　　　Tune: *Villa du Havre*

When peace, like a river, attendeth my
　way,
When sorrows, like sea-billows, roll;
Whatever my lot, Thou hast taught me to say,
"It is well, it is well with my soul!"

　　It is well with my soul,
　　It is well, it is well with my soul!

But, Lord, 'tis for Thee, for Thy coming, we
　wait;
The sky, not the grave, is our goal:
O trump of the angel! O voice of the Lord!
Blessèd hope! blessèd rest of my soul!

HORATIO GATES SPAFFORD

CHARLES HADDON SPURGEON

Spurgeon, Charles Haddon (Kelvendon, England, June 19, 1834—London, Jan. 31, 1892).
Charles Haddon Spurgeon has been rightly described as the Prince of Preachers, but he was also a hymn-writer of considerable ability. He published a hymn book for use in his congregation and contributed 20 of his own compositions.

Spurgeon was of Dutch origin, his family had fled for refuge to England during the six year persecution of Christians by the Duke of Alva in the sixteenth century. Saved in boyhood, he joined the Baptist Church at Isleham, and later became pastor in New Park St. Baptist Church, where Dr. John Rippon had been a former minister.

Great crowds were attracted by his unique presentation of the Gospel and soon it was necessary to erect a larger building. In 1861, the famous Metropolitan Tabernacle was opened in London, with seating capacity for six thousand. For many years the church was crowded, often an hour before the appointed time of the service. Two of Spurgeon's hymns are in the Believers Hymn Book. The best known being: "Amidst us our Beloved stands". This delightful hymn has for its scriptural background the appearance of the Lord Jesus in the Upper Room following His resurrection. Spurgeon was a world famous preacher, yet his contribution to hymnody was also outstanding, specially in the publishing of his twenty Psalm versions in 1866.

AMIDST US OUR BELOVED STANDS

Hymn 363　　　Tune: *Rivaulx*

Amidst us our Beloved stands
And bids us view His piercèd hands,
Points to His wounded feet and side,
Blest emblems of the crucified.

If now, with eyes defiled and dim,
We see the signs, but see not Him,
O may His love the scales displace
And bid us see Him face to face.

Thou glorious Bridegroom of our hearts,
Thy present smile a heaven imparts;
O lift the veil, if veil there be,
Let every saint Thy beauties see.

Come ye who bow to sovereign grace.................334
　　Hymn 334 was written compositely by Maria de Fleury and C.H. Spurgeon.

CHARLES HADDON SPURGEON

ANNE STEELE

Steele, Anne (Broughton, England, 1716—Broughton, 1778).

Anne Steele, like many other women hymn-writers was an invalid, confined to her room for the greater part of her life.

Her father was a timber merchant in Broughton, and he also was a local preacher, and a man who feared God. Anne Steele was saved and confessed Christ in baptism when she was fourteen years old.

The tragic drowning of the young man who was to marry her, on the day preceding their marriage, overshadowed her life. Following this sad event she began to write poems and spiritual hymns. These were signed by her nom-de-plume "Theodosia".

Anne Steele was the first English woman whose hymns appeared in extensive use in public singing.

"Father of mercies, in Thy Word" is her best known composition, and is still in constant use in assemblies of believers, expecially when gathered for Bible Study.

FATHER OF MERCIES IN THY WORD

Hymn 337   Tune: *Grafenberg*

Father of mercies! in Thy Word
What endless glory shines!
For ever be Thy Name adored
For these celestial lines.

Here the Redeemer's welcome voice
Spreads heavenly peace around;
And life and everlasting joys
Attend the blissful sound.

Divine Instructor! gracious Lord!
Thou art for ever near;
Teach us to love Thy sacred Word,
And view a Saviour there.

ANNE STEELE

JOSEPH STENNETT

Stennett, Joseph (Abingdon, England, 1663—London, England, 1713).

Joseph Stennett was one of the earliest of English hymn-writers. He had an excellent education at Wallenford Grammar School.

The Stennetts became known as England's greatest family in the realm of hymnody. Edward Stennett, the father of Joseph Stennett, was himself a hymn-writer. His grandson, also Joseph, had a son named Samuel, who was one of the outstanding preachers of his day and wrote a large number of hymns, including "Majestic sweetness sits enthroned upon the Saviour's brow". He also had a son named Joseph. All of them contributed hymns of faith.

Joseph Stennett, the first, wrote a number of hymns published in a small volume entitled *Hymns for the Lord's Supper*. One of these "O Blessed Saviour is Thy love" is still in extensive use.

O BLESSED SAVIOUR IS THY LOVE

Hymn 172   Tune: *Howard*

O Blessed Saviour! is Thy love
   So great, so full, so free?
Fain would we give our hearts, our minds,
   Our lives, our all, to Thee.

We love Thee for the glorious worth
   Which in Thyself we see;
We love Thee for the shameful Cross
   Endured so patiently.

O Lord! we treasure in our souls
   The memory of Thy love;
And ever may Thy Name to us
   A grateful odour prove.

JOSEPH STENNETT

SAMUEL STENNETT

Stennett, Samuel (Exeter, 1725—London, Aug. 24, 1795).

Dr. Samuel Stennett, the grandson of the writer of "O blessed Saviour! is Thy love, so great, so full, so free?" was saved in boyhood.

He became a Baptist minister at Lincoln Fields in London, at the age of twenty one. He was a man of outstanding personality and was one of the most influential preachers of his time. He was an advisor to many of the most distinguished statesmen in England, and was a personal friend of King George the third.

He was one of the greatest hymn-writers of the period, publishing some forty spiritual songs.

His greatest composition was the delightful hymn, which is worthy of its place in the Believers Hymn Book: "Majestic sweetness sits enthroned upon the Saviour's brow".

Samuel Stennett entitled this hymn "Chief among Ten Thousand" or "The Excellencies of the Lord Jesus", giving with it the Scripture reference, Song of Solomon, chapter 5 verses 10-16.

MAJESTIC SWEETNESS SITS ENTHRONED

Hymn 414   Tune: *Mirfield*

Majestic sweetness sits enthroned
  Upon the Saviour's brow;
His head with radiant glories crowned,
  His lips with grace o'erflow.

No mortal can with Him compare
  Among the sons of men;
Fairer is He than all the fair
  That fill the heavenly train.

He saw me plunged in deep distress,
  He came to my relief;
For me He bore the shameful cross,
  And carried all my grief.

Since from His bounty I receive
  Such proofs of love divine,
Had I a thousand hearts to give,
  Lord, they should all be Thine!

SAMUEL STENNETT

THOMAS STERNHOLD

Sternhold, Thomas (Blakeney, Glos., England, 1468—London, 1549).

Thomas Sternhold was a wealthy landowner having estates in Hampshire and Cornwall. He was a Gentleman of the King's Chamber, being the groom of the Royal Robes in the court of King Edward the sixth, the boy-King of England.

During the reign of King Edward, Sternhold authored a selection of 19 psalms in metre and obtained the patronage of the King for his work.

KING DAVID'S PSALM 103 IN METRE

Hymn 432

O thou, my soul, bless God the Lord;
　　And all that in me is
Be stirrèd up His holy name
　　To magnify and bless.

Bless, O my soul, the Lord thy God,
　　And not forgetful be
Of all His gracious benefits
　　He hath bestowed on thee:

Who doth redeem thy life, that thou
　　To death may'st not go down;
Who thee with loving kindness doth
　　And tender mercies crown.

THOMAS STERNHOLD

ALEXANDER STEWART

Stewart, Alexander (Glasgow, 1843—Prestwick, 1923).
Alexander Stewart was a lawyer with a large practice in the city of Glasgow, Scotland. He was awakened and saved when 19 years of age, and was in fellowship in the assembly at Union Hall for many years, before retiring to Prestwick.
He became an acceptable conference speaker and was often heard in Glasgow, Leominster, and London Bible Conventions.
As a hymn-writer he excelled in the writing of hymns concerning the Person of Christ and His present glories. Two of these are included in the Believers Hymn Book. The best known being "Lord Jesus Christ we seek Thy face".
Alexander Stewart went home after 60 years of fragrant testimony in his assembly life and in his professional life as a city lawyer. He never married, but gave both his material things and his time to the Lord's interests.

LORD JESUS CHRIST WE SEEK THY FACE

Hymn 129   Tune: *Retreat*

Lord Jesus Christ, we seek Thy face,
Within the veil we bow the knee;
O let Thy glory fill the place,
And bless us while we wait on Thee!

The brow that once with thorns was bound,
Thy hands, Thy side, we fain would see;
Draw near, Lord Jesus, glory-crowned,
And bless us while we wait on Thee.

O Lamb of God we lift our eyes,
  to Thee amidst the Throne 346

ALEXANDER STEWART

EDGAR PAGE STITES

Stites, Edgar Page (Cape, May, N.J. 1836—Cape, May, Jan. 7, 1921).

Edgar Stites was a retiring man by nature, but was an active Christian in personal testimony. He was a cousin of Eliza Hewitt, who wrote "More about Jesus would I know". Stites was a riverboat pilot for many years.

Ira D. Sankey relates in his book *Stories of Gospel Hymns* how he obtained the beautiful hymn of Stites "Simply trusting every day".

"The words were handed to me by D.L. Moody, in 1876, in the form of a newspaper clipping. He asked me could I write a tune for the beautiful words. I said, yes, providing that he would vouch for the doctrine taught in the verses. Moody said, most certainly. So I composed the music and sang the words which have been a blessing to many souls".

SIMPLY TRUSTING EVERY DAY

Hymn 248   Tune: *Trusting Jesus that is all*

Simply trusting every day,
Trusting through a stormy way;
Even when my faith is small,
Trusting Jesus, that is all.

Trusting Him while life shall last,
Trusting Him till earth is past,
Till within the jasper wall;
Trusting Jesus, that is all.

Trusting as the moments fly,
Trusting as the days go by;
Trusting Him whate'er befall,
Trusting Jesus, that is all.

EDGAR PAGE STITES

SARAH GERALDINE STOCK

Stock, Sarah Geraldine (London, England, Dec. 27, 1838—London, Aug. 29, 1898).

Sarah G. Stock devoted much of her time to the writing of children's books, and the authoring of hymns suitable for missionary meetings. Her God-given ability in these two realms was evident.

Her children's books included *Stories for the young from the Old Testament* and *A child's life of the Lord.*

Her fourteen hymns which were also published in a small volume *Joy in Sorrow* emphasises the great need of the field, which is the world. "O Master, when Thou callest, no voice may say Thee nay" was written for missionaries departing for India, and was first sung at a large Valedictory Service of the Zenana Society in London.

Two of her hymns are in the Believers Hymn Book.

LET THE SONG GO ROUND THE EARTH

Hymn 406   Tune: *Moel Llys*, by S.G. Stock

Let the song go round the earth,
  Jesus Christ is Lord!
Sound His praises, tell His worth,
  Be His name adored;
Every clime and every tongue
Join the grand, the glorious song.

Let the song go round the earth
  From the eastern sea,
Where the daylight has its birth,
  Glad, and bright, and free;
China's millions join the strains,
Waft them on to India's plains.

O Master when Thou callest 429

SARAH GERALDINE STOCK

JOHN HART STOCKTON

Stockton, John Hart (New Hope, Pa., U.S.A., April 19, 1813—Philadelphia, March 27, 1877).

John H. Stockton was converted at a Methodist meeting, and became a Methodist preacher in the New Jersey conference. He was gifted as a musician, and composer, as well as being the author of a number of well known hymns. His best known gospel hymn is still very popular "Come every soul by sin oppressed". Also included in the Believers Hymn Book is the beautiful hymn "The Cross, the Cross, the blood stained Cross."

John Hart Stockton was a personal friend of William Hunter, who was born in Ballymena, Northern Ireland, and wrote the hymn "The Great Physician now is near" for which Stockton wrote the suitable tune.

THE CROSS! THE CROSS!

Hymn 261   Tune: *The Cross* by J. Stockton

The Cross! the Cross! the blood-stained Cross!
  The Cross of Christ I see,
It tells me of that precious blood
  That once was shed for me.

The wrath! the wrath! the awful wrath
  That Jesus felt for me!
When bearing my sin's heavy load
  He died on Calvary.

The crown! the crown! the glorious crown!
  The crown of victory!
The crown of life! it shall be mine
  When I the Saviour see.

JOHN HART STOCKTON

SAMUEL JOHN STONE

Stone, Samuel John (Whitmore, Staffs., England, April 25, 1839—Charterhouse, England, Nov. 19, 1900).

Samuel John Stone was a man of firm convictions and strong personality. He was educated at Oxford University. Following his graduation he was ordained in the Church of England and became rector of a large parish in London, where he remained until his death.

Stone was a hymn-writer of high order and wrote over 50 hymns. His greatest composition "The Church's one foundation is Jesus Christ her Lord" is a foundation hymn of Christian faith.

The writing of this hymn in 1866 by Stone was on account of false teaching among Anglican bishops, especially John William Colenso, who denied the historic accuracy of the Pentateuch. Samuel Stone stood firm in the Faith and also stressed that the unity of the Church rested upon the recognition of the Lordship of Christ and not on the views of earthly leaders. These great truths he expressed in this hymn which originally had ten stanzas, but for hymnal purposes usually has four, in most books.

THE CHURCH'S ONE FOUNDATION

Hymn 449 Tune: *Aurellia*

The Church's one foundation
Is Jesus Christ her Lord:
She is His new creation
 By water and the word;
From heaven He came and sought her
 To be His holy bride;
With His own blood He bought her,
 And for her life He died.

Though with a scornful wonder
 Men see her sore oppressed,
By schisms rent asunder,
 By heresies distressed,
Yet saints their watch are keeping,
 Their cry goes up, How long?
And soon the night of weeping
 Shall be the morn of song.

SAMUEL JOHN STONE

HUGH STOWELL

Stowell, Hugh (Douglas, Isle of Man, Dec. 3, 1799—Salford, England, Oct. 8, 1865).

Hugh Stowell was a vicar in the Church of England, with a large parish at Salford. He was a faithful preacher of the Word, and had an unusual gift of so speaking that many were attracted to his services. Being evangelical he was a great soul-winner, and was specially owned of God.

Hugh Stowell was also a notable hymn-writer. A volume containing 46 of his hymns was published following his death. From this collection two have been chosen for the Believers Hymn Book: "From every stormy wind that blows" is a beautiful hymn on the comfort of prayer, at the mercy-seat. The other hymn so often sung "Jesus is our Shepherd" is couched in tender language exalting the gracious ministry of the Great Shepherd of His People.

THE MERCY SEAT

Hymn 50   Tune: *Retreat*

From every stormy wind that blows,
From every swelling tide of woes,
There is a calm, a safe retreat;
'Tis found beneath the Mercy-seat.

There is a place where Jesus sheds
The oil of gladness on our heads,
A place than all beside more sweet;
It is the blood-stained Mercy-seat.

There is a spot where spirits blend,
Where friend holds fellowship with friend;
Though sundered far, by faith we meet
Around one common Mercy-seat.

Jesus is our Shepherd, wiping every tear 109

HUGH STOWELL

JOSEPH SWAIN

Swain, Joseph (Birmingham, England, 1761—London, 1796).
Joseph Swain was left an orphan when only a child. He was an apprentice to an engraver. The pleasures of sin were his delight until God awakened him with thoughts of his sin and need. Not posessing a Bible, he purchased one, and read the Gospel by John, where he saw God's way of salvation and entered into the joy of everlasting life. He was twenty two years old when this change took place, but he only had twelve years to live the Christian life.

He began mission work in the slums of London, and saw some rescued from sin, and saved by grace. Joseph Swain had very little education, but he had ability as a poet and wrote over 200 hymns. These were published under the title *Walworth Hymns*. The best known of all his compositions is: "What will it be to dwell above, and with the Lord of Glory reign". He went home to be with the One of whom he wrote at the early age of thirty four.

O HOW THE THOUGHT THAT I SHALL KNOW

Hymn 347   Tune: *Farringdon*

O how the thought that I shall know
Jesus, who suffered here below
  To manifest God's favour;
For me and all the saints I love,
Both here and with Himself above,
Should my delighted spirit move
  At that sweet word, for ever.

For ever to behold Him shine,
For evermore to call Him mine,
  And see Him still before me;
For ever on His face to gaze,
And meet His full assembled rays,
While all his beauty He displays
  To all the saints in glory.

What will it be to dwell above, and with the Lord of
  Glory reign..355

JOSEPH SWAIN

THOMAS RAWSON TAYLOR

Taylor, Thomas Rawson (Ossett, Yorkshire, England, May 9, 1807—Bradford, England, March 15, 1836).

The name Thomas Rawson Taylor is almost unknown, but his hymn "Heaven is our Home" is well known. Very few hymns have the heavenly charm and beauty of this touching composition.

Taylor was a tender-hearted Christian, who never enjoyed health of body. This affecting hymn was written a few days before his death, at the early age of twenty-eight. He was greatly encouraged in his Christian life, and in writing hymns, by his personal friend James Montgomery, who admired his patience under trial and his potential as a writer of spiritual hymns.

I'M BUT A STRANGER HERE

Hymn 80   Tune: *Excelsior*

I'm but a stranger here;
  Heaven is my home!
Earth is a desert drear;
  Heaven is my home!
Danger and sorrow stand
Round me on ev'ry hand;
Heav'n is my fatherland,
  Heaven is my home!

Therefore I'll murmur not;
  Heaven is my home!
Whate'er my earthly lot;
  Heaven is my home!
For I shall surely stand
There at my Lord's right hand;
Heav'n is my fatherland:
  Heaven is my home!

THOMAS RAWSON TAYLOR

GERHARD TERSTEEGEN

Tersteegen, Gerhard (Mors, Westphalia, Nov. 1697— Muhliem, Prussia, April 3, 1769).

Gerhard Tersteegen was a silk-weaver by trade. He became a Christian, and gave up his business, opening his home to all who needed spiritual help. Many flocked to him for instruction in the Scriptures and his home became known as "The Pilgrim's Cottage." Tersteegen was a member of no sect, joined no church, lived a celibate, and spent most of his life in the retirement of his cottage.

His experience belongs to mystical history. He was a prolific hymn-writer composing one hundred and eleven hymns, fifty of these have been translated into English, one of which is included in the Believers Hymn Book. He is remembered as Germany's greatest hymnist.

THOU HIDDEN LOVE OF GOD

Hymn 290   Tune: *Stella*

Thou hidden love of God, whose height,
Whose depth unfathomed, no man knows,
I see from far Thy beauteous light,
And inly sigh for Thy repose:
My heart is pained, nor can it be
At rest till it finds rest in Thee.

Is there a thing beneath the sun
That strives with Thee my heart to share?
O tear it thence, and reign alone
The Lord of every motion there!
Then shall my heart from earth be free,
When it has found repose in Thee.

GERHARD TERSTEEGEN

THEODULF OF ORLEANS

Theodulf of Orleans. (Spain, 750—Angers, France, 821).
Theodulf, although a Spaniard, became an abbot of the Roman Catholic Church Monastery of Florence.
He was appointed Bishop of Orleans by Emperor Charlemange in 781. Theodulf was a faithful counselor and preacher to the Emperor. Following the Emperor's death, his son King Louis suspected Theodulf of treason, a charge of which he was innocent, and had him arrested and cast into prison at Angers. He died in 821, but whether a free man or a prisoner at the time of his death is uncertain. Some records show that he was poisoned in his cell. His stately Latin hymn "Gloria, Laus et Honour" was written one year before his death. The hymn originally had 78 lines. The five lines preserved in the Believers Hymn Book were translated by Sir Walter Shirley. They formed the chorus of the hymn.

GLORY, HONOUR, PRAISE AND POWER

Hymn 360   Tune: *Ashley*

Glory, honour, praise, and power,
Be unto the Lamb for ever;
Jesus Christ is our Redeemer,
Hallelujah! hallelujah!
Hallelujah! praise the Lord.

THEODULF OF ORLEANS

BOETHIA THOMPSON

Thompson, Boethia (Exeter, England, c.1865).

Concerning Boethia Thompson little information is available. She was a cousin of Antony Norris Groves. It is understood that her godly influence, and the testimony of her friend Mrs Paget, led to the conversion of Groves at Exeter.

Boethia Thompson wrote many beautiful hymns, specially suited for singing at the Lord's Supper. Some of these appear in *Hymns of Light and Love* under the name Mrs Thompson. Two of these hymns show the delight she had in the "breaking of bread": "Jesus Lord, we know Thee present, at Thy table freshly spread" and "O Lord it is Thyself to meet, to this sweet feast we come."

Although little is known of Boethia Thompson, she has left a spiritual legacy to the saints in her delightful hymns of communion and devotion. Five of these have an honoured place in the Believers Hymn Book.

O LORD IT IS THYSELF TO MEET

Hymn 427   Tune: *Land of Rest*

O Lord, it is Thyself to meet
  To this sweet feast we come;
Like Mary, resting at Thy feet
  We learn of Thee alone:
We well remember Thou hast said,
  This do, remembering Me;
So thus we take the wine, the bread,
  In memory of Thee.

O Lord, we come, for Thou art here;
  Enrich each memory;
Thy faithful promise brings Thee near
  And gathers us to Thee:
O body broken! poured out blood!
  Blest memories ever dear;
Thou Son of man! Thou Lamb of God!
  How good to meet Thee here!

Bride of the Lamb, there is for thee 29
I am watching for the morning 85
Jesus, Lord, I'm never weary 113
Jesus, Lord, we know Thee present.................... 114

BOETHIA THOMPSON

CENTRA THOMPSON

Thompson, Centra (Clapham, England, 1822—Clapham, 1909).

Centra Thompson resided with her life-long friend Jane Elwood at Clapham. Both of them wrote hymns and poetry which were published under the title *Songs of Praise*.

Centra Thompson's greatest contribution to hymnody "Gazing on Thee, Lord, in Glory" was first included in *Hymns for the Little Flock* 1881. It was chosen for the Believers Hymn Book in 1959.

The beautiful words extol the glories of the Lord Jesus, after His sufferings upon the Cross.

It is a special favourite in the assemblies of the Lord's people.

GAZING ON THEE, LORD, IN GLORY

Hymn 385   Tune: *West*

Gazing on Thee, Lord, in glory,
　While our hearts in worship bow,
There we read the wondrous story
　Of the cross, its shame and woe.

Every mark of dark dishonour,
　Heaped upon Thy thorn-crowned brow,
All the depths of Thy heart's sorrow
　Told in answering glory now.

Gazing on it we adore Thee,
　Blessèd, precious, holy Lord;
Thou, the Lamb, art ever worthy;
　This be earth's and heaven's accord.

CENTRA THOMPSON

W. NOEL TOMKINS

Tomkins, W, Noel (c.1865, England).

No information is available concerning this writer at this time. The only hymn known to be written by W. Noel Tomkins celebrates the glorious Resurrection of Christ, and the external results to all who are redeemed by His precious blood.

It is evident that the writer was in the enjoyment of the Person, worth, and work of the Saviour.

CHRIST'S GRAVE IS VACANT NOW

Hymn 32

Christ's grave is vacant now,
  Left for the throne above;
His Cross asserts God's right to bless,
  In His own boundless love.

'Twas there the blood was shed;
  'Twas there the life was poured;
There Mercy gained her diadem,
  While Justice sheathed her sword.

W. NOEL TOMKINS

AUGUSTUS MONTAGUE TOPLADY

Toplady, Montague Augustus (Farnham, England, Nov. 4, 1740—London, Aug. 4, 1778).
Augustus M. Toplady was the son of Major Richard Toplady who was killed in action, in Columbia, South America, while Augustus was an infant. He was educated at Trinity College, Dublin. While there he attended a gospel service in a barn at Codymain, where a Methodist lay preacher was conducting meetings. Recounting the incident Toplady stated that by the grace of God he was saved through resting upon the value of the precious blood of Christ.

Augustus Toplady began preaching shortly afterward and continued until his homecall at the early age of thirty eight.

He was a valuable contributor to hymnody. His greatest composition "Rock of Ages, cleft for me" has been translated into 300 languages. Authorities place it with three others, which are said to be the greatest hymns in the English language, i.e. "Wondrous Cross", "Coronation", "Jesus Lover of my soul".

ROCK OF AGES

Hymn 350   Tune: *Petra*

Rock of Ages! cleft for me,
Lo, I hide myself in Thee,
Where the water and the blood
From Thy wounded side which flowed
Are of sin the double cure,
Cleansing from its guilt and power.

Nothing in my hand I bring,
Simply to Thy cross I cling;
Naked, come to Thee for dress;
Helpless, look to Thee for grace;
Hungry, thirsty, still I flee,
All-sufficient Lord, to Thee.

A debtor to mercy alone 7
From whence this fear and unbelief 51
O precious blood, O glorious death 216
When languor and disease invade 320

AUGUSTUS MONTAGUE TOPLADY

SAMUEL PRIDEAUX TREGELLES

Tregelles, Samuel Prideaux (Falmouth, England, Jan. 3, 1813—Plymouth, April 24, 1875).

Samuel P. Tregelles was the son of a Quaker. He was possessed of great mental ability. He was educated at Falmouth Grammar School. When young he became a Christian and was early associated with brethren. For some years he studied the ancient manuscripts of the New Testament. After laborious studies he produced his Greek New Testament, which is a valuable asset to Bible students. He was recognised as one of the most distinguished Bible scholars of his day.

Samuel Tregelles also wrote a large number of hymns, all characterised by an exalted spiritual quality.

Six of his compositions are in the Believers Hymn Book.

THY BROKEN BODY, GRACIOUS LORD

Hymn 291   Tune: *Federal Street*

Thy broken body, gracious Lord,
Is shadowed by this broken bread:
The wine, which in this cup is poured,
Points to the blood which Thou hast shed.

Brethren! in Thee, in union sweet,
For ever be Thy grace adored!
'Tis in Thy Name that now we meet,
And know Thou'rt with us, gracious Lord.

Father! we, Thy children, bless Thee 46
Holy Saviour! we adore Thee 74
Lord Jesus, we believing 144
Thy name we bless, Lord Jesus........................ 287
The gloomy night will soon be past.................... 452

SAMUEL PRIDEAUX TREGELLES

GEORGE FREDERICK TRENCH

Trench, George Frederick (Stapleston, Ireland, 1841—Ardfert, Co. Kerry, Ireland, Nov. 11, 1915).

George F. French was the son of Fitz-John Trench, a cavalry officer in the British Army. He became concerned about his eternal welfare listening to the solemn preaching of Gratton Guinness in Merrion Hall, Dublin. He became a Christian shortly afterwards. At Trinity College, Dublin, where he was educated, he became friendly with a student who helped him greatly in the things of God, and who later became Sir Robert Anderson, K.C.B., L.L.B. This friendship continued for over fifty years. George Trench evangelised in fellowship with such well-known brethren as Denham Smith, F.C. Bland, Harry Moorhouse, and Lord Congleton. He made his home at Ardfert Abbey, Co. Kerry, where the believers gathered in assembly fellowship to "break bread" in the Granary, on his estate.

George F. Trench was a diligent student, an able preacher, and wrote a number of books. His best known being: *After the Thousand Years* and *The Life that is Life indeed*. As a hymn-writer he was not so well known, but one beautiful composition is preserved in the Believers Hymn Book.

COME, YE SAINTS, REJOICE WITH JESUS

Hymn 321   Tune: *Confidence*

Come, ye saints, rejoice with Jesus,
Called with Him His joy to share;
Seraphs worship, angels praise Him;
We His friends and followers are:
  Lost ones found and
  Dead ones raisèd,
Now the heart of Jesus cheer.

Praise Him! praise Him! never ceasing,
Ye who prove God's boundless grace:
Have we asked, and has He answered?
Thankful hearts to heaven raise:
  He is worthy
  To receive His children's praise.

GEORGE FREDERICK TRENCH

JANETTA A. TRENCH

Trench, Janetta A. (Dublin, Jan. 31, 1843—Dublin, June 14, 1925).

Janetta Trench (*nee* Taylor) was saved while very young. She was married in 1866 to John Alfred Trench, a personal friend and associate of J.N. Darby and J.G. Bellett. The Trench's were known for their godliness and faithfulness in the assembly in Dublin. Janetta Trench wrote the beautiful hymn "Buried in the grave of Jesus" on the occasion of her own baptism. The hymn has been ascribed the first place among hymns on believer's baptism.

Mrs Trench wrote a number of devotional hymns in which she expressed her love to the Person of the Lord Jesus. Her most famous lines are:

"Lord Jesus, Thou alone art worthy,
Ceaseless praises to receive,
For Thy love and grace and goodness,
Rise o'er all our thoughts conceive."

BURIED IN THE GRAVE OF JESUS

Hymn 21   Tune: *Stuttgart*

Buried in the grave of Jesus,
  We believe what God has said;
Faith, His judgment acquiescing,
  Reckons now that we are dead.

Death and judgment are behind us,
  Grace and glory are before;
All the billows rolled o'er Jesus,
  There exhausted all their power.

Jesus died, and we died with Him,
  Buried in His grave we lie,
One with Christ in resurrection,
  Seated now in Him on high.

Lord, we share in Thy rejection,
  Thy reproach, O may we love;
Here we stand in Thine acceptance
  In the Father's sight above.

JANETTA A. TRENCH

H.L. TURNER

Turner, H.L. (U.S.A. c.1860).
Details concerning this writer are unknown.
The hymn: "It may be at morn" first appeared under the name H.L. Turner and the tune written by James McGranahan in *Gospel Hymns, No.3*. The title of the hymn was given as "Christ Returneth" and the Scriptural reference: "I will come again" (John 14:1-3). The date given for the hymn is 1878.

IT MAY BE AT MORN

Hymn 106

It may be at morn,
When the day is awaking,
When sunlight through darkness
And shadow is breaking,
That Jesus will come
In the fulness of glory,
To receive from the world His own.

O Lord Jesus, how long?
How long—ere we shout the glad song?
Christ returneth! Hallelujah!
Hallelujah! Amen!
Hallelujah! Amen!

H.L. TURNER

EDWARD WAKEFIELD

Wakefield, Edward (Kendal, England, 1804—Kendal, 1870). Edward Wakefield was saved while young. With Henry Groves (Antony Norris Groves eldest son), Henry Dyer and others an assembly was formed in Kendal. Edward Wakefield was a very influential man. He was the bank manager in Kendal. In 1834 he became one of the first trustees in supporting the building of a large house to be the first orphan home by George Muller. He and James Wright were in constant fellowship in the work at Ashley Down. Later a larger orphanage was built to accommodate over 2,000 orphans, as well as the staff. George Muller, James Wright (Muller's son-in-law), Edward Wakefield, and other brethren joined in prayer for the needed funds to operate this great work. They asked nothing from any, but made known their need to God alone. Over one million pounds passed through their hands for orphans and over four hundred thousand pounds for Bibles and Mission work. There were times of need and trials. During one such occasion Edward Wakefield wrote his hymn; "Press forward and fear not." In 1851 Wakefield built a Gospel Hall in Kendal and handed it to the brethren for use as the gathering place of the assembly.

The writer was invited to speak to the orphans at Ashley Down in 1955. It was a never to be forgotten experience.

PRESS FORWARD AND FEAR NOT

Hymn 235   Tune: *St. Denio*

Press forward and fear not!
 The billows may roll,
But the power of Jesus
 Their rage can control:
Though waves rise in anger,
 Their tumult shall cease;
One word of His bidding
 Shall hush them to peace.

Press forward and fear not!
 Though trials be near;
The Lord is our refuge,
 Whom, then, shall we fear?
His staff is our comfort,
 Our safeguard His rod;
Then let us be steadfast
 And trust in our God.

EDWARD WAKEFIELD

MARY JANE DECK WALKER

Walker, Mary Jane Deck (Bury-St-Edmunds, April 27, 1816—Cheltenham, July 2, 1878).
Mary Jane Deck Walker was the sister of James G. Deck, who wrote many hymns in the Believers Hymn Book, and was well known among brethren. She married Dr. Edward Walker, of Cheltenham. Many of Mary Walker's hymns were first printed as leaflets, but later were published as *Psalms and Hymns of Worship*, by Dr. Walker in 1855. She wrote "The wanderer no more shall roam" as a complement to Charlotte Elliot's hymn "Just as I am", which was written nine years earlier, and already had received wide acceptance. She also wrote the well known hymn "I have Christ, what want I more".

One of her choicest hymns is still a favourite among believers everywhere "I journey through a desert drear and wild".

Her greatest hymn, which has gained unbounded favour, and has been used in many conversions is "Jesus I will trust Thee". This hymn was a favourite of Francis Ridley Havergal. It is said that she quoted the first verse a few minutes before she passed away.

After the death of her husband in 1872 Mary J. Walker spent her remaining years in fellowship with the believers in assembly fellowship at Cheltenham.

I JOURNEY THROUGH A DESERT DREAR AND WILD

Hymn 92   Tune: *Toulon*

I journey through a desert drear and wild,
Yet is my heart by such sweet thoughts
    beguiled
Of Him on whom I lean, my Strength, my
    Stay,
I can forget the sorrows of the way.

Thoughts of His sojourn in this vale of tears;
The tale of love unfolded in those years
Of sinless suffering and patient grace,
I love again and yet again to trace.

O Spotless Lamb of God in Thee 217
The wanderer no more will roam 286

MARY JANE DECK WALKER

ANNA LAETITIA WARING

Waring, Anna Laetitia (Neath, S. Wales, April 19, 1820—Clifton, Bristol, England, May 10, 1910).

Anna Laetitia Waring had many sufferings to endure, which she bore patiently. The words of one of her hymns expresses her thoughts concerning her sufffering:

"Who would not suffer pain like mine,
To be consoled like me?"

God spared her for many years. Her ninety years were a blessing to all who had the privilege of knowing her, leaving behind a legacy of 40 beautiful hymns and a number of delightful poems. Anna Waring was also a Hebrew student. Her later years, spent near Bristol, were fruitful, as she engaged in helping discharged prisoners, especially women, back to normal life, and to guide them to the Saviour.

Her hymn "In heavenly love abiding" is included in the Believers Hymn Book.

IN HEAVENLY LOVE ABIDING

Hymn 395   Tune: *Penlon*

In heavenly love abiding,
  No change my heart shall fear;
And safe is such confiding,
  For nothing changes here:
The storm may roar without me,
  My heart may low be laid,
But God is round about me,
  And can I be dismayed?

Green pastures are before me
  Which yet I have not seen;
Bright skies will soon be o'er me
  Where dark the clouds have been:
My hope I cannot measure,
  My path to life is free;
My Saviour has my treasure,
  And He will walk with me.

ANNA LAETITIA WARING

SAMUEL MILLER WARING

Waring, Samuel Miller (Alton, England, March 1792—Bath, Sept. 19, 1827).

Samuel Miller Waring was the uncle of Anna Laetitia Waring. His short life of 35 years, was a fruitful one. His hymns were published in a small volume *Sacred Melodies*". Two of his hymns are in the Believers Hymn Book.

UNTO HIM WHO LOVED US

Hymn 307

Unto Him who loved us, gave us
    Every pledge that love could give;
Freely shed His blood to save us;
    Gave His life that we might live;
      Be the kingdom,
      And dominion,
    And the glory evermore!

Now to Him who loved us, gave us..................... 465
    (the last doxology in the B.H.B.)

SAMUEL MILLER WARING

ANNA BARTLETT WARNER

Warner, Anna Bartlett (New York, 1820—New York, 1915).

Anna Bartlett Warner is the writer of the children's hymn: "Jesus loves me this I know". It has been stated that this hymn is sung in more languages than any other, and has been widely used in the salvation of many children. Using her pseudonym, Amy Lathrop, Anna Bartlett Warner published a large number of hymns and spiritual songs. For many years she conducted Bible Study Groups for the Military Cadets at West Point.

When she died at the age of 95, she was buried with full military honours by the order of the President. The beautiful strains of "Jesus loves me this I know" were played by the Military Band at the cemetery.

All her hymns are marked by great simplicity, depth of meaning, and beauty of diction.

O EYES THAT ARE WEARY

Hymn 182   Tune: *Clarendon Street*

O eyes that are weary, and hearts that are sore,
Look off unto Jesus and sorrow no more;
The light of His countenance shineth so bright,
That on earth, as in heaven, there need be no night.

Soon, soon shall I know the full beauty and grace
Of Jesus, my Lord, when I stand face to face;
I shall know how His love went before me each day,
And wonder that ever my eyes turned away.

ANNA BARTLETT WARNER

ISAAC WATTS

Watts, Isaac (Southampton, England, July 17, 1674—London, November 25, 1748).

Isaac Watts was educated at the Nonconformist Academy of Thomas Rowe, Stoke Newington, near London. He was converted while only a boy. For twelve years he preached in Mark Lane Independent Church in London. During a serious illness Sir Thomas Abney invited him to stay at his mansion house in Hertfordshire. Isaac Watts remained with the Abney family the rest of his life, acting as tutor to the children, and chaplain to the household. During this time he devoted himself to writing hymns and books. One of his books *Logic* was used as a textbook in Oxford University. Universally acclaimed as the "Father of English Hymnody" he wrote over 600 hymns. Many appeared in his famous collection *Hora Lyricae*. Isaac Watts believed that the New Testament Church should sing praise to God in the "language of the New Testament".

Some consider "The Wondrous Cross" as the finest hymn in the English language. It has been printed in more hymn books than any other.

After his death a monument honouring Watts was erected in Westminster Abbey. Eleven of his hymns are included in the Believers Hymn Book.

WHEN I SURVEY THE WONDROUS CROSS

Hymn 322　　　Tune: *Deep Harmony*

When I survey the wondrous Cross
On which the Prince of Glory died,
My richest gain I count but loss,
And pour contempt on all my pride.

See from His head, His hands, His feet,
Sorrow and love flow mingled down;
Did e'er such love and sorrow meet,
Or thorns compose so rich a crown?

Alas and did my Saviour bleed 6
Come let us join our joyful songs 38
Not all the blood of beasts 170
O God our help in ages past 207
Unto the Lamb that once was slain 308
With joy we meditate the grace 326
Join all the glorious names 342
Blest be the everlasting God 369
Blest morning whose first dawning rays 370
Jesus shall reign where'er the sun 403

ISAAC WATTS

C. ANNE WELLESLEY

Wellesley, C. Anne (England, 1850—1910).
Little information is obtainable concerning this hymn-writer. Like many other women she has left a hymn of true worship which, like Mary's ointment, has filled many an assembly with the fragrance of His Name, and the sweetness of His song.

Anne Wellesley was associated with brethren gathered in the Name of the Lord Jesus. She was a translator of hymns from French to English. One of her translations included in the Believers Hymn Book is Dr. Rossier's "Lord e'en to death Thy love could go."

Her own contribution to the hymn book is an outstanding composition which is exceedingly precious to saints who gather unto the Name of the Lord Jesus: "Gathered to Thy Name Lord Jesus."

GATHERED TO THY NAME, LORD JESUS

Hymn 384   Tune: *Chapel Brae*

Gathered to Thy Name, Lord Jesus,
   Losing sight of all but Thee,
O what joy Thy presence gives us,
   Calling up our hearts to Thee.

Loved with love which knows no measure
   Save the Father's love to Thee,
Blessèd Lord, our hearts would treasure
   All the Father's thoughts of Thee.

O the joy, the wondrous singing
   When we see Thee as Thou art;
Thy blest name, Lord Jesus, bringing
   Sweetest music to God's heart.

Notes of gladness, songs unceasing,
   Hymns of everlasting praise,
Psalms of glory, joy increasing
   Through God's endless day of days.

C. ANNE WELLESLEY

CHARLES WESLEY

Wesley, Charles (Epworth, England, Dec. 18, 1707—London, England, Mar. 29, 1788).
Charles Wesley was the youngest of nineteen children. Three of the Wesley brothers were outstanding hymn-writers i.e. Samuel, John and Charles. Charles exceeded them all being the author of over 7,000 hymns. Their mother was a very godly woman whose influence upon her family was such that all nineteen of them were finally saved by grace. In 1737, when Charles Wesley was thirty years of age, he was led to faith in Christ for salvation through the preaching of Count Nicolaus Zinzendorf. The first hymn he wrote following his conversion was "O for a thousand tongues to sing". John and Charles Wesley travelled on horseback throughout England, preaching the gospel to throngs of people, and thousands were brought to the Lord as Saviour. The best known hymn of Charles Wesley "Jesus, Lover of my soul" is considered by authorities to be among the four greatest hymns in the English language the others being: "Rock of Ages" (Toplady); "Wondrous Cross" (Watts); and "Coronation" (Perronet).

JESUS LOVER OF MY SOUL

Hymn 119   Tune: *Hollingside*

Jesus, Lover of my soul,
  Let me to thy bosom fly,
While the billows near me roll,
  While the tempest still is high:
Hide me, O my Saviour, hide
  Till the storm of life is past;
Safe into the haven guide,
  O receive my soul at last.

Blest be the dear uniting love 25
Head of the Church 67
My God I am Thine 153
O for a thousand tongues 191
O Love divine how sweet 203
Our souls are in God's mighty hand 221
And can it be that I should gain 365
Lo He comes with clouds 408
Love divine all loves excelling 413
My heart is full of Christ 420
Put thou thy trust in God 440
Rejoice the Lord is King 441
Ye servants of God 464

CHARLES WESLEY

JOHN WESLEY

Wesley, John (Epworth, England, June 17, 1703—London, March 2, 1791).

John Wesley and Charles Wesley are known as the founders of Methodism. The life and labours of John Wesley are truly incredible. It is recorded that he travelled over a quarter of a million miles on horseback, preaching over 40,000 times, resulting in thousands of conversions. He was one of the most active men in his day, rising every morning for prayer at four o'clock, never wasting an hour of any day until he retired at ten o'clock. He wrote many large volumes, translated numerous hymns from four langauges, as well as composing 27 original hymns. His chief contribution to hymnody was the editing of his brother Charles' hymns, which in all were 7,000.

Like his brother Charles, John was brought to the full assurance of faith in Christ through words spoken to him by Count Zinzendorf. One of his hymns is included in the Believers Hymn Book, also his translation of Wolfgang C. Deszler's great hymn "O come, Thou stricken Lamb of God".

LORD JESUS, THY GREAT LOVE TO ME

Hymn 141   Tune: *Colchester* (by his brother Samuel)

Lord Jesus, Thy great love to me
  No thought can reach, no tongue declare:
O bend my wayward heart to Thee,
  And reign without a rival there;
Thine, wholly Thine, alone I'd live,
Myself to Thee entirely give.

In suff'ring be Thy love my peace,
  In weakness be Thine arm my strength;
And when the storms of life shall cease,
  And Thou from heaven wilt come at length,
Lord Jesus, then this heart shall be
For ever satisfied with Thee.

O come, Thou stricken Lamb of God 180
Written by Wolfgang C. Deszler. Translated by John Wesley.

JOHN WESLEY

MARY WHATELY

Whately, Mary (Dublin, Ireland, 1824—Cairo, Egypt, 1889).

Mary Whately was the daughter of Richard Whately, the Archbishop of Dublin, who also was a hymn writer of note. Mary Whately was a devoted Christian and desired to establish a school for girls in Egypt, with emphasis placed on the teaching of the Bible. After investing much time, energy, and money the school was opened in Cairo. On a visit in 1869 by the Prince of Wales, he was so impressed with her work that he arranged a more suitable place for a new school to be erected, and granted a subsidy. The new school proved to be a place where girls came in large numbers to be educated, and to hear the plain teaching of the Gospel, which resulted in the conversion of many of these young people.

Mary Whately was also a talented writer of poems and hymns. One of her outstanding compositions was incorporated into Sankey's collection which he set to a suitable tune. This hymn is preserved in the Believers Hymn Book. At her death Mary Whately was honoured by the city of Cairo for her work in the school.

O THEY'VE REACHED THE SUNNY SHORE

Hymn 348   Tune *Song of Praise* (Ira Sankey)

O they've reached the sunny shore
They will never suffer more,
All their pain and grief are o'er,
    Over there.

O the street is shining gold,
And the glory is untold;
'Tis our Shepherd's peaceful fold,
    Over there.

O they never shed a tear,
For the Lord Himself is near,
And to Him they're ever dear,
    Over there.

MARY WHATELY

RICHARD WHATELY

Whatley, Richard (London, England, Feb. 1, 1787—Dublin, Oct. 8, 1863).

Richard Whately was educated at Oxford University, where he had a brilliant career as a student. He was ordained as a Church of England minister and later became the Archbishop of Dublin. His three daughters were all hymn-writers i.e. Emma Jane, Blanche, and Mary. In 1860 Whately published an interesting book on *Prayer*. One of his hymns became very popular as a result: "He sitteth o'er the waterfloods".

HE SITTETH O'ER THE WATERFLOODS

Hymn 73   Tune: *Tallis 'Ordinal*

He sitteth o'er the waterfloods,
   And He is strong to save;
He sitteth o'er the waterfloods,
   And guides each drifting wave.

He sitteth o'er the waterfloods,
   As in the days of old,
When o'er the Saviour's sinless head
   The waves and billows rolled.

He sitteth o'er the waterfloods;
   Then doubt and fear no more,
For He who passed through all the storms
   Has reached the heavenly shore.

RICHARD WHATELY

FREDERICK WHITFIELD

Whitfield, Frederick (Threapwood, England, Jan. 7, 1814—Croydon, England, Sept. 13, 1904).

Frederick Whitfield was educated at Trinity College Dublin, Ireland. He became a Church of England minister and spent most of his life in Hastings. Frederick Whitfield was evangelical in his preaching, and his life was marked by devotion to Christ and humility of spirit. He was a prolific writer and published thirty volumes of prose and verse containing many of his well known hymns.

Hymns concerning the Name of the Lord Jesus have always held a prominent place in the affections of Christians: Mary Peter's "O Lord how much Thy Name unfolds" and John Newton's "How sweet the Name of Jesus sounds" are examples. Frederick Whitfield has also contributed two beautiful hymns which extol the Saviour's precious Name: "Jesus, O Name of power divine" and "There is a Name I love to hear". The other hymns he wrote also give an unfolding of the glory and beauty of the Person of Christ. Four of his hymns are in the Believers Hymn Book.

THERE IS A NAME I LOVE TO HEAR

Hymn 285   Tune: *Belmont*

There is a Name I love to hear,
I love to speak its worth;
It sounds like music in mine ear,
The sweetest Name on earth.

It tells me of a Saviour's love,
Who died to set me free;
It tells me of His precious blood,
The sinner's perfect plea.

I need Thee precious Saviour 95
I saw the Cross of Jesus 97
Jesus! O Name of power divine 116

FREDERICK WHITFIELD

JOHN GREENLEAF WHITTIER

Whittier, John Greenleaf (Haverhill, Mass. U.S.A., Dec. 17, 1807—Hampton Falls, New Hampshire, U.S.A., Sept. 7, 1892).

John Greenleaf Whittier is accepted by hymnologists as "America's greatest lyrical and most distinguished poet". Although he never wrote hymns, many of his beautiful poems have been used as hymns. Whittier was born into a farming family of Quakers. He had a modest education, but from his earliest years had a great delight in writing poetry. When he was seventeen his sister sent some of his verse to William Garrison, editor of the Newbury Free Press, who was a famous abolitionist. Garrison was so impressed with the quality of the poem that he made the journey to the farm to meet the youthful writer. He encouraged him to make journalism his profession. Whittier became a renowned journalist and was editor of the New England Weekly Review in 1831. He adopted the cause of the slaves and was elected Secretary of the American Anti-Slavery Society. His excellent and touching poems on the evil of slavery gained him the title of the "Poet Laureate of Abolition". Whittier, who never married, was a Quaker of the old school, always wearing the garb of the Society of the Friends. The Quakers did not sing hymns at their services, yet one of them has given us the most beautiful hymns of the Christian Church.

DEAR LORD AND FATHER OF MANKIND

Hymn 377   Tune: *Repton*

Dear Lord and Father of mankind,
   Forgive our foolish ways;
Reclothe us in our rightful mind;
In purer lives Thy service find,
   In deeper reverence, praise.

In simple trust like theirs who heard,
   Beside the Syrian sea,
The gracious calling of the Lord,
Let us, like them, without a word
   Rise up and follow Thee.

JOHN GREENLEAF WHITTIER

WILLIAM WHITTINGHAM

Whittingham, William (Chester, England, 1524—Durham, 1579).

William Whittingham was a student of repute, in his day, being educated at Brasenore College and the University of Orleans, France. He was appointed to draw up a Service Manual which contained 51 psalms which he had turned into metre. On the basis of his metre of Psalm 23, Francis Rous produced the final composition of that great Psalm of King David.

THE LORD'S MY SHEPHERD

Hymn 454   Tune: *Crimond*

The Lord's my Shepherd, I'll not want:
He makes me down to lie
In pastures green; He leadeth me
  The quiet waters by.

Written compositely by
WILLIAM WHITTINGHAM & FRANCIS ROUS

MAJOR DANIEL WEBSTER WHITTLE

Whittle, Daniel Webster (Chicopee Falls, Mass., U.S.A. Nov. 22, 1840—Northfield, Mass., March 4, 1901).

Daniel Webster Whittle was employed in his mid-teens as a cashier of the Wells Fargo Bank in Chicago. He served as a Lieutenant, in the 72nd Illinois Light Infantry in the Civil War, and was severely wounded at Vicksburg, which resulted in the loss of an arm. As he lay in hospital he recalled his mother, on the morning of his departure for the war, had given him a New Testament, which had remained unopened at the bottom of his haversack. He now took the precious Book and while reading John 3:16 was brought to faith in the Son of God and was saved. Later he was promoted to the rank of major, and was known as Major Whittle the rest of his life. Following the war he was treasurer of the Elgin Watch Company in Chicago, but resigned in 1873 to become an evangelist. In 1878 he conducted gospel meetings in Scotland and Ireland. In Belfast large companies thronged his services and a large number were saved. He began writing hymns in 1877 using the pen-name of "El Nathan". His hymns had for their theme the Blessed Hope of the Second Coming of the Lord Jesus. His best known composition being: "The Crowning Day" and "Jesus is Coming". Characterised by their scriptural teaching, the hymns of Major Whittle were widely adopted by evangelists, and were in constant use, even as they are today.

Besides the hymns already mentioned, other of his familiar hymns are: "There shall be showers of blessing", "Come believing", "Redemption ground" and "I know whom I have believed".

WE SHALL MEET WITH OUR LOVED ONES AGAIN

Hymn 28   Tune: *Blessed Hope*

Blessed hope that in Jesus is given,
  In our sorrow to cheer and sustain,
That soon with our Saviour in heaven
  We shall meet with our loved ones again.

  Blessed hope! ... Blessed hope! ...
  We shall meet with our loved ones again.

Blessed hope! how it shines in our sorrow,
  Like the star over Bethlehem's plain,
That it may be, with Him, ere the morrow,
  We shall meet with our loved ones again.

Jesus is coming! Sing the glad word! 112
Our Lord is now rejected 223
Come sing my soul and praise the Lord 335

MAJOR DANIEL WEBSTER WHITTLE

FANNY THEODORA WIGRAM

Wigram, Fanny Theodora (England—Montreal, March 1871).

Fanny Theodora Wigram was the daughter of George Vicesimus Wigram, who was the twentieth child of Sir Robert Wigram, this being the reason for his middle name, which means twenty in Latin.

Fanny Theodora Wigram's father compiled *The Englishman's Greek and English Concordance of the New Testament* and *The Englishman's Hebrew and Chaldee Concordance of the Old Testament*. He also edited the magazine *Present Testimony* and *Hymns for the little Flock*.

Fanny Theodora Wigram travelled with her father in his labours among the assemblies, especially in the West Indies and Guiana, where they spent some years. Being a nurse she used her skills in helping the sick and needy in the various places where her father preached the gospel.

She wrote one beautiful hymn of worship which is included in the Believers Hymn Book.

WORTHY OF HOMAGE AND OF PRAISE

Hymn 462   Tune: *Angel's Song*

Worthy of homage and of praise;
Worthy by all to be adored;
Exhaustless theme of heavenly lays;
Thou, Thou art worthy, Jesus Lord.

Now seated on Jehovah's throne,
The Lamb once slain, in glory bright;
'Tis thence Thou watchest o'er Thine own,
Guarding us through the deadly fight.

Yet, Saviour, Thou shalt have full praise;
We soon shall meet Thee on the cloud,
We soon shall see Thee face to face,
In glory praising as we would.

FANNY THEODORA WIGRAM

KATE BARCLEY WILKINSON

Wilkinson, Kate Barcley (England, 1859—1928).
Very little information is available concerning this writer. She was active in work among girls and young women, and also had responsible interest in the Keswick Convention.
The only hymn from her pen is included in the Believers Hymn Book.

MAY THE MIND OF CHRIST MY SAVIOUR

Hymn 416   Tune *Grenofen*

May the mind of Christ my Saviour
Live in me from day to day,
By His love and power controlling
All I do and say.

May the word of God dwell richly
In my heart from hour to hour
So that all may see I triumph
Only through His power.

May the peace of God my Father
Rule my life in everything,
That I may be calm to comfort
Sick and sorrowing.

KATE BARCLEY WILKINSON

WILLIAM WILLIAMS

Williams, William (Ceyn-y-Coed, Wales, 1717—Pantycelyn, Wales, Jan. 11, 1791).

William Williams was, in the realm of hymnody, to Wales what Isaac Watts was to England. He wrote over 300 hymns in his native Welsh language, and became known as "The sweet singer of Wales". This greatest hymn was translated by himself into English "Guide us, O Thou Great Jehovah" and is found in most hymn books including the Believers Hymn Book.

Williams was born into a lonely farmhouse in Wales, where he died seventy four years later. As a young man, about to take a medical career, he heard Howell Harris, a well known Methodist, preach the gospel faithfully. From that time his life was changed. He became a curate of the Church of England, but went from place to place preaching the gospel in association with George Whitefield. The Bishop was displeased and reprimanded Williams. Undaunted, he left the parish and went forth to evangelise for the next forty five years of his life. His preaching was owned of God in the salvation of hundreds of his fellow Welshmen.

He is best remembered by the hymn "Guide us, O Thou Great Jehovah" which has been sung worldwide, and used on many historic and moving occasions.

The original hymn as it was written in the Welsh language is as follows:

"Arglwdd, arwain trwy'r anialwch
Fi, bererin qwael ei wedd
Nad oes ynof nerth na bywyd
Fel yn gor wedd yn y bedd
Hollalluog
Ydyw'r un a'm cwyd i'r lan."

GUIDE US, O THOU GREAT JEHOVAH

Hymn 60   Tune: *Cum Rhondda*

Guide us, O Thou great Jehovah,
Pilgrims through this barren land;
We are weak, but Thou art mighty;
Hold us by Thy powerful hand:
Bread of heaven,
Feed us now and evermore.

Saviour, come! we long to see Thee,
Long to dwell with Thee above;
And to know, in full communion,
All the sweetness of Thy love:
Come, Lord Jesus!
Take Thy waiting people home.

Saviour lead us by Thy power 444

WILLIAM WILLIAMS

ELLEN H. WILLIS

Willis, Ellen H. (c.1872).
Records concerning Ellen H. Willis are not available.
David Beattie writes in *Romance of Sacred Song*:
"I left it all with Jesus, long ago" an old fashioned hymn, which has brought much consolation to needy souls, is not to be found in many present day hymnals. Written by Ellen H. Willis it first appeared in Ira D. Sankey's earliest collection of hymns."
The beautiful hymn with its old English Melody is in the Believers Hymn Book, and is still sung in many gatherings of the saints.

ALL WITH JESUS

Hymn 94

I left it all with Jesus long ago;
All my sins I brought Him, and my woe:
When by faith I saw Him on the tree,
Heard His still, small whisper, "'Tis for thee,"
From my heart the burden rolled away:
        Happy day!

I leave it all with Jesus day by day;
Faith can firmly trust Him, come what may:
Hope has dropped her anchor, found her rest
In the calm, sure haven of His breast;
Love esteems it heaven to abide
        At His side.

ELLEN H. WILLIS

CATHERINE WINKWORTH

Winkworth, Catherine (London, England, Sept. 13, 1827—Monretier, France, July 1, 1878).

Catherine Winkworth lived in Manchester England, before moving to reside in Clifton, near Bristol. She was a pioneer in the higher education of young women, being the Governess of the Red Maid's School in Bristol for many years. She was also one of the founders of Clifton High School for girls.

In the realm of hymnology she has a notable place on account of her ability as a translator. From the German hymns of Franck, Weiss, Nicolia and Neander she published *Chorale Book for England* 1863, also *Great singers of Germany* 1869.

Perhaps her greatest work was translating Joachim Neander's hymn "Praise to the Lord, the Almighty, the King of Creation".

Dr. John Julian describes this as "a magnificent hymn of praise to God, and of the first rank in its class". Neander, who died at the early age of thirty, wrote the hymn over 200 years before it was translated into English by Catherine Winkworth.

PRAISE TO THE LORD

Hymn 439   Tune: *Lobe Den Herren*

Praise to the Lord, the Almighty, the
  King of creation;
O my soul, praise Him, for He is thy health
  and salvation;
    All ye who hear,
    Brethren and sisters draw near,
    Praise Him in glad adoration.

Praise to the Lord, O let all that is in me
  adore Him;
All that hath life and breath come now with
  praises before Him;
    Let the Amen
    Sound from His people again:
    Gladly for aye we adore Him.

Written compositely by
JOACHIM NEANDER & CATHERINE WINKWORTH

JOHN WITHY

Withy, John (Gloucester, England, Oct. 2, 1809—Bristol, 1882).

John Withy was of such a retiring nature that even his family did not know of some of the hymns he had written, until after his death.

Withy was associated with the brethren in Bethesda assembly in Bristol, a gathering where George Muller, Henry Craik, and many other prominent teachers were in fellowship.

For many years before his homecall John Withy passed through times of intense suffering. It was during this time that many of his greatest hymns were written.

The writer had the privilege of preaching in Bethesda, where the fragrant memories of these godly men of other days still remain.

John Withy's wedding hymn, included in the Believers Hymn Book, is still a favourite, chosen by many young couples to be sung on their wedding day.

LORD JESUS LET THY FAVOUR REST

Hymn 136   Tune: *Heathside*

Lord Jesus, let Thy favour rest
  Upon this bond of love;
May it be bound in heaven, and bliss
  With blessing from above.

Thy ways, Thou heavenly Bridegroom, be
  The pattern for this pair;
Their constant springs be found in Thee,
  Their life Thy love declare.

And when the day of light shall shine,
  Their work approvèd be;
Thou then with joy wilt own as Thine,
  Whate'er was done to Thee.

JOHN WITHY

CHRISTOPHER WORDSWORTH

Wordsworth, Christopher (Lambeth, England, Oct. 30, 1807—Harwood, England, March 21, 1885).

Christopher Wordsworth was a nephew of the well known poet William Wordsworth. He was educated at Winchester School and at Cambridge University, where he was a distinguished scholar and an outstanding athlete. He was ordained in the Church of England in 1833, and served as Headmaster at Harrow. His only parochial charge was a little country parish in Berkshire, with the unique name of Stanford-in-the-Vale-Cum-Goosey. He remained there for twenty years. While there he realised that his parishioners attended church more for what they could receive in material benefits such as coal, blankets, etc. Wordsworth thought of the words of the Lord Jesus "It is more blessed to give than to receive", so to teach his people a lesson he wrote the beautiful words of his greatest hymn "O Lord of heaven and earth and sea". Christopher Wordsworth was not only a hymn writer, but being an outstanding scholar he wrote a very valuable commentary on the whole Bible. The particular value of this work is that he used Scripture to interpret Scripture. Records of his life state that he was a man of devotion to Christ, sound in the Faith, and marked by humility.

O LORD OF HEAVEN AND EARTH AND SEA

Hymn 426   Tune: *Almsgiving*

O Lord of heaven and earth and sea,
To Thee all praise and glory be:
How shall we show our love to Thee
    Who givest all?

Thou didst not spare Thine only Son,
But gav'st Him for a world undone,
And freely with that blessèd One
    Thou givest all.

We lose what on ourselves we spend;
We have as treasure without end
Whatever, Lord, to Thee we lend,
    Who givest all.

CHRISTOPHER WORDSWORTH

W. YERBURY

Yerbury, W. (died 1863).
Information concerning this hymn-writer is not recorded further than a short reference by Dr. John Julian, the famous hymnologist:

"The hymns of W. Yerbury were published posthumously, but no date is available. One or two of these are included in brethren hymn books, including "Thy love we own Lord Jesus."

THY LOVE WE OWN LORD JESUS

Hymn 295 Tune: *Cyprus*

Thy love we own, Lord Jesus;
In service unremitting,
Within the veil Thou dost prevail,
Each soul for worship fitting.
Encompassed here with failure,
Each earthly refuge fails us;
Without, within, beset with sin,
Thy Name alone avails us.

Thy love we own, Lord Jesus!
Thy way is traced before Thee;
Thou wilt descend, and we ascend,
To meet in heavenly glory.
Soon shall the blissful morning
Call forth Thy saints to meet Thee,
Only our Lord, alone adored,
With gladness then we'll greet Thee.

W. YERBURY

COUNT NICOLAUS LUDWIG ZINZENDORF

Zinzendorf, Nicolaus Ludwig Count (Dresden, Germany, May 26, 1700—Herrnhut, Saxony, May 9, 1760).

Count Zinzendorf's father was Prime Minister at the Saxon Court, but died shortly after the Count was born. His mother and grandmother were godly women, so he was early acquainted with the Word of God and, like Timothy, was influenced to become a Christian by his home background. He was educated at Wittenburg University where he studied law. Later he held a court appointment but resigned to go forth and preach the Gospel. His estate became the refuge for the persecuted people of Moravia, and he became a real Shepherd to them, ministering not only from his material wealth, but imparting spiritual instruction. On grounds of being unorthodox he was banished from his estate at Herrnhut, and Saxony. He then travelled establishing colonies of Moravians in Switzerland, England, Holland, North America, and the West Indies. Through his ministry the Wesleys were brought to the assurance of salvation through faith in Christ alone. The government of Saxony finally allowed him to return to Herrnhut in 1748, where he remained until his death. Count Zinzendorf was a prolific hymn writer, composing over 2,000 hymns, thirty six of these have been translated into English. His best known hymn being "Jesus, the Lord our Righteousness" and is included in the Believers Hymn Book.

JESUS, THE LORD OUR RIGHTEOUSNESS

Hymn 120   Tune: *Fulda*

Jesus, the Lord our Righteousness!
Our beauty Thou, our glorious dress;
'Midst flaming worlds, whilst thus arrayed,
With joy shall we lift up our head.

Bold shall we stand in that great day,
For who aught to our charge shall lay?
While by Thy blood absolved we are
From sin's tremendous curse and fear.

COUNT NICOLAUS LUDWIG ZINZENDORF

Selected Bibliography

Bailey, Albert E. *The Gospel in Hymns.* New York: Charles Scribners, 1950.

Benson, Louis F. *The English Hymn.* New York: George Doran, 1915.

Brown, Theron & Butterworth. *The story of hymns and tunes.* New York: George Doran, 1906

Beattie, David J. *Stories of our hymns and writers.* Scotland: John Ritchie, 1934.

Chapman, Robert Cleaver. *Hymns and Meditations.* Glasgow: Pickering & Inglis, 1900.

Colquhoun, Frank. *A Hymn Companion.* Hodder & Stoughton: London, 1985.

Cope, Henry F. *Hymns you ought to know.* London: Fleming Revell, 1906.

Colson, Elizabeth. *Hymn Stories.* Boston: The Pilgrim Press, 1925.

Deck, James G. *Hymns and Sacred Poems.* Heijkoop: Netherlands, 1889.

Flint, Ann Johnstone. *Poems.* Evangelical Publishers: Toronto.

Fox Etelle... *Hymns of Canadian Interest.* Etchcraft: Toronto.

Gabriel, Charles... *The singer and thier songs.* Rodeheaver Co., 1915.

Hart, J. *Biography of Gospel Hymns.* Partridge: London, 1886.

Hall, J.H. *Know your hymns.* Boston: Wilde Co., 1944.

Hostetler, Lester. *Handbook to Mennonite hymns.* Newton: Kansas, 1949.

Hustad, Don. *Hymns for the Living Church.* Illinois: Hope Press, 1978.

Julian, John. *A Dictionary of Hymnology.* New York: Scribners, 1892.

Knapp, C. *Who wrote our hymns?* Denver: Wilson Foundation, 1925.

Laufer, Calvin W. *Hymn Lore.* Westminster Press, 1932.
Macmillan, Alexander. *Hymns of the Church.* Toronto: United Church Publishing House, 1935.
Mable, Norman. *Popular Hymns and their writers.* Independent Press, 1946.
Moffatt & Patrick. *Handbook to the Church Hymnal.* London: Oxford Press, 1927.
Moyer, E.S. *Wycliffe Biographical.* Moody Press.
Osbeck, Kenneth. *101 Hymn Stories (2 Vols.)* Grand Rapids: Kregel Press.
Paul K. *Victorian Hymnody.* London: French & Co., 1881.
Parry, K. *Christian Hymns.* London: S.C.M. Press.
Prescott, J.E. *Christian Hymn writers.* Cambridge, 1883.
Reynolds, William. *A survey of Christian Hymnody.* New York: Holt, Rinehart & Winston, 1963.
Routley, Erik. *Hymns today and tomorrow.* New York: Abingdon Press, 1964.
Rizk, Helen. *Stories of Christian Hymns.* Abingdon Press.
Roach, Adrian. *The Little Flock Hymn Book.* Morganville, N.J.: Present Truth Pub.
Sankey, Ira D. *The story of Gospel Hymns.* New York: Harper Publishers, 1906.
Sanville, George W. *Forty Gospel Hymn Stories.* Rodeheaver, Hall, Mack, Co., 1943.
Smith, Oswald J. *Hymn Stories.* Winona Lake: Rodeheaver Co., 1963
Stebbins, George. *Gospel Hymn Stories.* George Doran Co., 1924.
Thompson, Ronald. *Who's Who of Hymn Writers.* London: Epworth Press, 1967.
Wake, Arthur N. *Companion for Christian Worship.* St. Louis: Bethany Press, 1970.

General Reference Works

Encyclopaedia Britannica.
The Witness. Henry Pickering, Glasgow, Vols. 55-60.
The Believers Magazine. John Ritchie, Kilmarnock. Vols. 29-34.
Truth & Tidings. Toronto, Vol. 2-9 (Hymns by Hector Alves).
Dictionary of National Biography.
Curiosities of Literature (article on Psalms) 1882.

Index

First line	No. in B.H.B.	Authors	Page
A debtor to mercy alone	7	Aug. M. Toplady	379
A little while, our Lord shall come	14	James G. Deck	115
A mind at perfect peace with God	3	Catesby Paget	289
A pilgrim through this lonely world	11	Sir Edward Denny	117
A Rock that stands for ever	9	Paul Gerhardt	157
Abba, Father, we adore Thee	2	Robert Hawker	185
Abba, Father, we approach Thee	1	James G. Deck	115
Abide in me, my Saviour	362	E. Costello	7
According to Thy gracious Word	5	James Montgomery	257
Alas, and did my Saviour bleed	6	Isaac Watts	399
All hail the power of Jesus' Name	361	Edward Perronet	293
All that I was, my sin, my guilt	8	Horatius Bonar	61
All the way my Saviour leads me	364	Francis van Alystyne (F. Crosby)	11
Amidst us our Beloved stands	363	Charles H. Spurgeon	343
And can it be that I should gain	365	Charles Wesley	403
And is it so! we shall be like	366	John Nelson Darby	109
Around Thy grave, Lord Jesus	13	James G. Deck	115
Around Thy table, Holy Lord	4	Mary Peters	295
As sinners saved we gladly	12	James H. Evans	137
Assembled, Lord, at Thy behest	367	David J. Beattie	29
Awake, and sing the song	368	William Hammond	177
Awake, my soul, in joyful lays	10	Samuel Medley	245
Before the throne of God above	15	Charitie L. Bancroft	21
Begone unbelief, my Saviour	27	John Newton	283
Behold a Spotless victim dies	16	Anonymous	13
Behold, behold the Lamb of God	30	Joseph Hoskins	197
Behold the Lamb with glory	17	Thomas Kelly	211
Behold the throne of grace	18	John Newton	283
Behold what love	26	Robert Boswell	63
Beneath the Cross of Jesus	23	Eliz. C. Clephane	91
Blessed be God our God	24	Horatius Bonar	61
Blessed Hope that in Jesus is	28	Daniel W. Whittle	417
Blessed Lord our souls	19	Mary Peters	295
Blest be the dear uniting love	25	Charles Wesley	403
Blest be the everlasting God	369	Isaac Watts & William Cameron	75

First line	No. in B.H.B.	Authors	Page
Blest morning, whose first dawning	370	Isaac Watts	399
Break every barrier down	371	Bertha Mullen	269
Break Thou the bread of life	373	Mary Lathbury	221
Brethren let us join to bless	20	John Cennick	81
Bride of the Lamb, there is for thee	29	Boethia Thompson	373
Bright, bright home beyond	22	H.K. Burlingham	73
Bright with all His crowns	31	Sir Edward Denny	117
Buried in the grave of Jesus	21	Janetta A. Trench	385
By Christ redeemed, in Christ	372	George Rawson	309
Christ has done the mighty work	33	Horatius Bonar	61
Christ the Lord is risen on high	37	Anonymous	13
Christ's grave is vacant now	32	W. Noel Tomkins	377
Christians, go and tell of Jesus	35	E.P. Hammond	175
Cling to the Mighty One	36	Henry Bennett	36
Come, all ye saints of God	34	James Boden	59
Come, every joyful heart	375	Samuel Stennett	249
Come, let us all unite to sing	39	Howard Kingsbury	217
Come, let us join our cheerful songs	38	Isaac Watts	399
Come, let us sing the matchless	40	Samuel Medley	245
Come, my soul, thy suit prepare	374	John Newton	283
Come, sing my soul and praise	335	Daniel W. Whittle	417
Come, Thou fount of every blessing	43	Robert Robinson	315
Come ye saints, rejoice	321	George F. Trench	383
Come ye that know	41	George Burder	71
Come ye who bow to sovereign	334	Maria de Fleury	121
Crown Him with many crowns	376	Matthew Bridges	67
Crowned with thorns upon the Tree	42	Grattan Guinness	169
Crowns of glory ever bright	44	Thomas Kelly	211
Dear Lord and Father	377	John G. Whittier	413
Done is the work that saves	45	Horatius Bonar	61
Endless praises to our Lord	336	Thomas Kelly	211
Eternal Light! eternal Light	378	Thomas Binney	51
Faint not Christian	47	James H. Evans	137
Far, far away, in heathen darkness	379	James McGranahan	275
Farewell for the present	358	C. Russell Hurditch	201
Father of mercies! in Thy Word	337	Anne Steele	345
Father of peace, and God of love	380	Philip Doddridge	125
Father, we, Thy children bless	46	S.P. Tregelles	381
Fight the good fight	381	John S.B. Monsell	255
Forever with the Lord	48	James Montgomery	257
For the bread and for the wine	49	Horatius Bonar	61
From every stormy wind that blows	50	Hugh Stowell	363
From Greenland's icy mountains	382	Reginald Heber	187
From whence this fear and unbelief	51	A.M. Toplady	379

First line	No. in B.H.B.	Authors	Page
Gathered, Lord, around Thy table	383	Douglas Russell	321
Gathered to Thy name, Lord Jesus	384	C. Ann Wellesley	401
Gazing on Thee, Lord, in glory	385	Centra Thompson	375
Glory, glory everlasting	52	Thomas Kelly	211
Glory, honour, praise	360	Theodulf of Orleans	371
Glory to God on high	56	Thomas Kelly	211
Glory to Thee Thou Son of God	386	Edward C. Quine	305
Glory unto Jesus be	54	Archd. Rutherford	323
Go labour on	387	Horatius Bonar	61
God is love, His word has said it	357	Thomas Kelly	211
God moves in a mysterious way	53	William Cowper	99
God's almighty arms are round me	57	Joseph D. Smith	337
Grace 'tis a charming sound	55	Philip Doddridge	125
Gracious God we worship Thee	388	S. Trevor Francis	149
Great God of wonders	58	Samuel Davies	113
Great Shepherd of Thy chosen flock	59	John Newton	283
Guide us, O Thou great Jehovah	60	William Williams	423
Hail, Thou once despised Jesus	61	John Bakewell	19
Hail, to the Lord's Anointed	389	James Montgomery	257
Happy they who trust in Jesus	62	Thomas Kelly	211
Hark! hark! hear the glad	327	Anonymous	13
Hark! how the blood-bought	338	John Kent	215
Hark! my soul, it is the Lord	63	William Cowper	99
Hark! ten thousand voices crying	65	John Nelson Darby	109
Hark! 'tis the watchman's cry	64	Anonymous	13
Have ye counted the cost	66	Jane E. Leeson	225
He comes, Emmanuel comes	68	James G. Deck	115
He dies! He dies! the lowly Man	390	C. Russell Hurditch	201
He giveth more grace	391	Annie J. Flint	147
He leadeth me, O blessed thought	70	Joseph H. Gilmore	161
He lives, the great Redeemer	71	Anne Steele	345
He sitteth o'er the waterfloods	73	Richard Whately	409
Head of the Church triumphant	67	Charles Wesley	403
Heirs of salvation	69	H.K. Burlingham	73
Here o'er the earth	72	Anonymous	13
Here, O our Lord, we see Thee	339	Horatius Bonar	61
Holy, holy, holy! Lord God	392	Reginald Heber	187
Holy Saviour, we adore Thee	74	Samuel P. Tregelles	381
Hope of our hearts, O Lord	75	Sir Edward Denny	117
How bright that blessed hope	76	Anonymous	13
How firm a foundation	77	Richard Keene	209
How good is the God we adore	78	Joseph Hart	179
How I praise Thee, precious Saviour	393	Mary E. Maxwell	243
How sweet the Name of Jesus	79	John Newton	283
I am a stranger here	82	Anonymous	13
I am the Lord's! O joy	394	Lucy A. Bennett	35

First line	No. in B.H.B.	Authors	Page
I am Thine, O Lord	329	Frances van Alystyne	11
I am waiting for the dawning	81	S. Trevor Francis	149
I am watching for the morning	85	Boethia Thompson	373
I bless the Christ of God	86	Horatius Bonar	61
I bow me to Thy will, O God	87	Frederick W. Faber	139
I have a home above	89	Henry Bennett	33
I have been at the altar	88	Amelia M. Hull	199
I hear the accuser roar	93	Samuel W. Gandy	155
I hear the words of love	91	Horatius Bonar	61
I heard the voice of Jesus say	90	Horatius Bonar	61
I journey through a desert	92	Mary Jane D. Walker	391
I left it all with Jesus, long ago	94	Helen W. Willis	425
I need Thee, precious Saviour	95	Frederick Whitfield	411
I once was a stranger	96	R. Murray McCheyne	273
I saw the Cross of Jesus	97	Frederick Whitfield	411
I thirst, but not as once I did	98	William Cowper	99
I was a wandering sheep	105	Horatius Bonar	61
I will never, never leave thee	330	Anonymous	13
I will sing of my Redeemer	102	Philip P. Bliss	55
I would commune with Thee	100	George B. Bubier	69
I'm a pilgrim and a stranger	83	Mary S.B. Dana	107
I'm but a stranger here	80	Thomas R. Taylor	367
I'm waiting for Thee, Lord	84	H.K. Burlingham	73
I've found a Friend	103	James G. Small	335
I've found a joy in sorrow	104	Jane Crewdson	103
I've found the precious Christ	107	John Mason	239
Immortal, invisible, God only	396	Walter C. Smith	339
In heavenly love abiding	395	Ann L. Waring	393
In seasons of grief	99	John Price	303
In the Name of Jesus every knee	397	Caroline M. Noel	285
Is it Thy will that I should be	340	Anonymous	13
It may be at morn	106	H.L. Turner	387
It passeth knowledge	101	Mary Shekleton	329
Jehovah is our strength	108	Samuel Barnard	23
Jesus calls us o'er the tumult	398	C. Frances Alexander	9
Jesus Christ, Thou King of Glory	110	H.K. Burlingham	73
Jesus! I am resting, resting	400	Jean S. Piggott	301
Jesus in His heavenly temple	111	R. Cleaver Chapman	85
Jesus is coming, sing the glad word	112	Daniel W. Whittle	417
Jesus is our Shepherd	109	Hugh Stowell	363
Jesus, Lord, I'm never weary	113	Boethia Thompson	373
Jesus, Lord, I need Thy presence	399	George Goodman	163
Jesus, Lord, we come together	401	T.H. Reynolds	313
Jesus, Lord, we know Thee present	114	Boethia Thompson	373
Jesus, lover of my soul	119	Charles Wesley	403
Jesus, O name of power divine	116	Frederick Whitfield	411
Jesus, our Lord, with what joy	402	H. D'Arcy Champney	83

First line	No. in B.H.B.	Authors	Page
Jesus shall reign	403	Isaac Watts	399
Jesus, source of life eternal	115	Ernst C. Homburg	193
Jesus, the Christ! eternal Word	341	Morshead	263
Jesus, the Lord, our righteousness	120	Count N. Zinzendorf	435
Jesus, Thou joy of loving hearts	404	Bernard of Clairvaux	291
Join all the glorious names	342	Isaac Watts	399
Joy, joy, joy, there is joy	117	Anonymous	13
Just as I am, Thine own to be	405	Marianne Farningham	141
Just as I am, without one plea	333	Charlotte Elliott	133
Just as Thou art, how wondrous fair	118	J. Denham Smith	337
Kept, safely kept	121	William Blane	53
Lamb of God, our souls adore	122	James G. Deck	115
Lamb of God, Thou now art seated	123	James G. Deck	115
Let the song go round the earth	406	Sarah G. Stock	357
Let us love and sing and wonder	124	John Newton	283
Let us rejoice in Christ	125	John Newton	283
Light of the world, shine on	343	Edward Bickersteth	47
Like a river, glorious	407	Frances R. Havergal	181
Lo, He comes! with clouds	408	J. Cennick & C. Wesley	403
Look upon us, blessed Lord	411	T. Clausnitzer & R. Macalister	271
Look, ye saints, the sight	127	Thomas Kelly	211
Lord, accept our feeble song	126	Thomas Kelly	211
Lord, dismiss us with Thy blessing	132	John Fawcett	143
Lord, e'en to death Thy love	409	Dr. H.L. Rossier	313
Lord Jesus, are we one	128	James G. Deck	115
Lord Jesus Christ, the thought	137	Bernard of Clairvaux	39
Lord Jesus Christ, we seek Thy face	129	Alexander Stewart	353
Lord Jesus, come	130	George Jekel	207
Lord Jesus, friend unfailing	131	S.C. Gottfried Kuster	219
Lord Jesus, I love Thee	134	W.R. Featherstone	145
Lord Jesus, in Thy name alone	135	Mary Peters	295
Lord Jesus, let Thy favour rest	136	John Withy	429
Lord Jesus, my Savour, how vast	133	Anonymous	13
Lord Jesus, Thine	138	Albert Midlane	247
Lord Jesus, Thou who only art	140	Anonymous	13
Lord Jesus, Thy great love	141	John Wesley	405
Lord Jesus, to tell of Thy love	142	Thomas Haweis	183
Lord Jesus, we believing	144	Samuel P. Tregelles	381
Lord Jesus, who didst once appear	146	John Berridge	43
Lord, speak to me that I may speak	410	Frances R. Havergal	181
Lord, Thy word abideth	412	Henry W. Baker	17
Lord, to Thee, my heart	139	Elizabeth Codner	93
Lord, we are Thine	143	James G. Deck	115
Lord, we would ne'er forget	148	James G. Deck	115

First line	No. in B.H.B.	Authors	Page
Love divine, all loves excelling	413	Charles Wesley	403
Low in the grave He lay	344	Robert Lowry	231
Majestic sweetness sits	414	Samuel Stennett	249
Man of Sorrows, what a Name	147	Philip P. Bliss	55
Master, speak! Thy servant	415	Frances R. Havergal	181
May the grace of Christ	145	John Newton	283
May the mind of Christ	416	Kate B. Wilkinson	421
Meeting in the Saviour's Name	149	Thomas Kelly	211
Mid the splendours of the glory	150	William Reid	311
Midst the darkness, storm and	155	Paul Gerhardt	157
Mine eyes are unto Thee	417	F.J.M. (F. van Alystyne)	11
More about Jesus	418	Eliza E. Hewitt	189
My chains are snapt	152	Margaret L. Carson	77
My days are gliding swiftly by	151	David Nelson	281
My glorious Victor, Prince	419	Handley C.G. Moule	265
My God, I am Thine	153	Charles Wesley	403
My God, I have found	157	J. Denham Smith	337
My God, my Father	165	Charlotte Elliott	133
My God, what cords of love	154	Philip Doddridge	125
My heart is full of Christ	420	Charles Wesley	403
My hope is built on nothing less	158	Edward Mote	267
My Redeemer! O what beauties	159	Anonymous	13
My rest is in heaven	160	Henry F. Lyte	233
My Saviour, whom absent	161	William Cowper	99
My Shepherd is the Lamb	156	John Beaumont	31
My sins were laid on Jesus	166	Horatius Bonar	61
My soul amid this stormy world	164	Robert C. Chapman	85
My tongue shall spread	163	Anonymous	13
No blood, no altar now	171	Horatius Bonar	61
No bone of Thee was broken	167	Robert C. Chapman	85
No condemnation, O my soul	162	Robert C. Chapman	85
No gospel like this feast	421	Elizabeth R. Charles	87
Not all the blood of beasts	170	Isaac Watts	399
Now I have found a Friend	168	Henry J. Hope	195
Now in a song of grateful	169	Samuel Medley	245
Now to Him who loved us	465	Samuel M. Waring	395
O blessed God, how kind	181	John Kent	215
O blessed Lord, what hast Thou	173	Mary Peters	295
O blessed Saviour, is Thy love	172	Joseph Stennett	247
O blessed Saviour, who but Thee	174	Sir Edward Denny	117
O Christ, He is the fountain	190	Anne Ross Cousin	97
O Christ, in Thee my soul hath	178	B.E. (Emma Bevan)	45
O Christ, Thou heavenly Lamb	179	C. Russell Hurditch	201
O Christ, Thou Son of God	423	William H. Bennett	37
O Christ, we rest in Thee	175	James G. Deck	115

443

First line	No. in B.H.B.	Authors	Page
O Christ what burdens bowed	176	Anne Ross Cousin	97
O Christian, awake.	177	Anonymous	13
O come Thou stricken Lamb	180	Wolfgang C. Deszler	119
O eyes that are weary	182	Anna B. Warner	397
O for a thousand tongues to sing	191	Charles Wesley	403
O for the peace that floweth	192	Jane Crewdson	103
O for the robes of whiteness	193	Charitie L. Bancroft	21
O God of Bethel!	422	J. Logan & P. Doddridge	229
O God of matchless grace.	185	H.K. Burlingham	73
O God, our help in ages past	207	Isaac Watts	399
O gracious Lord, be with us	183	Sir Edward Denny	117
O happy day that fixed.	188	Philip Doddridge	125
O happy day when first we felt.	189	James G. Deck	115
O Head once filled with bruises	187	Paul Gerhardt	157
O Holy Saviour, friend unseen	194	Charlotte Elliot	133
O how the thought that I shall	347	Joseph Swain	365
O Jesus Christ, grow Thou in me	424	Johann C. Lavater	223
O Jesus, I have promised	425	John E. Bode	57
O joy of the justified	186	Frank Bottome	65
O Lamb of God, still keep me	197	James G. Deck	115
O Lamb of God, 'tis joy to know	196	James G. Deck	115
O Lamb of God, we lift our eyes	346	Alexander Stewart	353
O Lord, how much Thy name	201	Mary Peters	295
O Lord, I would delight in Thee	200	John Ryland	325
O Lord, it is Thyself to meet	427	Boethia Thompson	373
O Lord of heaven and earth	426	Chris. Wordsworth	431
O Lord, Thy love's unbounded	206	John Nelson Darby	109
O Lord, 'tis joy to look above	199	James G. Deck	115
O Lord, when we the path retrace	202	James G. Deck	115
O Lord, where'er Thy people	204	William Cowper	99
O Lord, who art Thy people's	198	Sir Edward Denny	117
O Lord, who now art seated	205	James G. Deck	115
O Love divine, how sweet	203	Charles Wesley	403
O Love, that will not let me go	428	George Matheson	241
O Master! when Thou callest	429	Sarah G. Stock	357
O our Saviour, crucified!	210	Robert C. Chapman	85
O patient, spotless One	215	C.A. Bernstein	41
O precious blood	216	A.M. Toplady	379
O safe to the Rock	345	William O. Cushing	105
O spotless Lamb of God, in Thee	217	Mary Jane D Walker	391
O teach us more	195	James Hutton	203
O the bitter shame and sorrow!	430	Theodore Monod	253
O the deep, deep love of Jesus	431	S. Trevor Francis	149
O they've reached the sunny	348	Mary Whately	407
O thou, my soul, bless God	432	Thomas Sternhold	351
O Thou spotless Lamb of God	218	James G. Deck	115
O Thou whose bounty	332	Jane Crewdson	103

First line	No. in B.H.B.	Authors	Page
O what a lonely path were	208	Sir Edward Denny	117
O what a Saviour	209	James McGranahan	275
O what shall we feel	225	Emily Grimley	167
O wondrous hour	433	Sir Edward Denny	117
O worship the King	434	Sir Robert Grant	165
Of Thee, Lord, we would never tire	184	Mary Peters	295
On Christ salvation rests	212	Samuel Medley	245
On that same night, Lord Jesus	435	George West Fraser	151
On Thy broken body feeding	214	Mary Carter	79
Once more before we part	211	J. Hart & R. Hawker	179
One there is above all others	213	Marianne Nunn (Elizabeth Dark)	111
Our blest Redeemer ere He breathed	436	Harriet Auber	15
Our Father, O what gracious ways	219	Anonymous	13
Our Father, we would worship	220	Anonymous	13
Our great Redeemer liveth!	437	Fanny Hope (F. van Alystyne)	11
Our Lord is now rejected	223	Daniel W. Whittle	417
Our souls are in God's mighty hand	221	Charles Wesley	403
Our times are in Thy hand	222	William F. Lloyd	227
Ours are peace and joy divine	224	William Reid	311
Peace, what a precious sound	227	John F. Elwin	135
Poor, weak and worthless	349	John Newton	283
Praise God from whom all blessings	359	Thomas Ken	213
Praise Him, Praise Him	226	Frances van Alystyne	11
Praise, my soul, the King	438	Henry F. Lyte	233
Praise, praise ye the name	228	Horatius Bonar	61
Praise the Lord, and leave	229	William G. Sloan	233
Praise the Lord who died	232	Thomas Kelly	211
Praise the Saviour, ye who	233	Thomas Kelly	211
Praise Thy Saviour, O my soul	230	Anonymous	13
Praise to the Lord, the Almighty	439	J. Neander & C. Winkworth	279, 427
Praise ye the Lord, again, again	236	Mary Peters	295
Prayer is the soul's sincere desire	234	James Montgomery	257
Precious is the blood	231	Gordon Furlong	153
Press forward and fear not	235	Edward Wakefield	389
Put thou thy trust in God	440	Paul Gerhardt & C. Wesley	157, 403
Rejoice, rejoice, ye saints	237	C. Russell Hurditch	201
Rejoice! the Lord is King	441	Charles Wesley	403
Rejoice, ye saints, the time	240	Anonymous	13
Revive Thy work, O Lord	242	Albert Midlane	247
Rise my soul, behold 'tis Jesus	238	J. Denham Smith	337
Rise my soul, thy God directs thee	239	J. Nelson Darby	109
Rise up and hasten!	241	J. Denham Smith	337
Rock of Ages	350	A.M. Toplady	379

First line	No. in B.H.B.	Authors	Page
Safe in the arms of Jesus	243	Frances van Alystyne (F. Crosby)	11
Salvation to our God	246	Mary Peters	295
Saviour, again to Thy dear Name	442	John Ellerton	131
Saviour, lead us by Thy power	444	William Williams	423
Saviour, more than life to me	244	Frances van Alystyne (F. Crosby)	11
Saviour, through the desert	254	Thomas Kelly	211
Saviour, Thy dying love	443	Sylvanus D. Phelps	297
Saviour, Thy name I love	245	James G. Deck	115
Saviour, we remember Thee	251	S. Trevor Francis	149
Simply trusting every day	248	Edgar Page Stites	355
Son of God 'twas love	250	Anonymous	13
Sound the high praises	247	Thomas Moore	259
Sovereign grace o'er sin	249	John Kent	215
Speak, Lord, in the stillness	445	E. May Crawford (Grimes)	101
Sun and Shield, O Lord	255	Horatius Bonar	61
Sweet are the seasons	253	Anonymous	13
Sweet feast of love divine	252	Sir Edward Denny	117
Sweet is the savour	256	Anonymous	13
Sweet the moments rich in blessing	258	Sir Walter Shirley	331
Sweeter sounds than music knows	257	John Newton	283
Take my life, and let it be	446	F. Ridley Havergal	181
Take the world, but give me Jesus	259	Frances van Alystyne F. Crosby)	11
Teach me Thy way, O Lord	447	B. Mansell Ramsey	307
The atoning work is done	260	Thomas Kelly	211
The bread and wine are spread	448	George Goodman	163
The Church's one foundation	449	Samuel John Stone	361
The cloudless day is nearing	262	C.A.H.	7
The countless multitude on high	265	Archd. J. Rutherford	323
The cross! the blood-stained cross	261	John Hart Stockton	359
The cross! the Christian's only glory	264	A.B. McKay	249
The day of glory bearing	266	John George Deck	115
The day Thou gavest, Lord, is	450	John Ellerton	131
The gloomy night will soon be past	452	Samuel P. Tregelles	381
The glory shines before me	263	H.K. Burlingham	73
The God of Abraham praise	273	Thomas Olivers	287
The gospel of Thy grace	267	Arthur T. Pierson	299
The happy morn is come	268	Dr. Thomas Haweis	183
The head that once with thorns was	269	Thomas Kelly	211
The holiest now we enter	270	Mary Peters	295
The King of love my Shepherd is	451	Henry W. Baker	17
The Lamb of God to slaughter led	271	Robert C. Chapman	85
The Lord Himself shall come	272	James Montgomery	257
The Lord is risen indeed	275	Thomas Kelly	211

First line	No. in B.H.B.	Authors	Page
The Lord is risen: now death's dark	277	William P. McKay	277
The Lord of glory, who is He	276	Robert C. Chapman	85
The Lord will perfect that which	453	Winifred A. Iverson	205
The Lord's my Shepherd	454	Wm. Whittingham & F. Rous	319
The love that Jesus had for me	282	Jane E. Hall	173
The night is far spent	284	Thomas Kelly	211
The night is wearing fast away	278	Miss Hoare	191
The Saviour lives	280	Samuel Medley	245
The sorrows of the daily life	281	Anonymous	13
The veil is rent	283	James G. Deck	115
The wanderer no more shall roam	286	Mary J. Walker	391
There is a fold	279	John East	127
There is a fountain	274	William Cowper	99
There is a green hill	455	C. Frances Alexander	9
There is a Name	285	Frederick Whitfield	411
This world is a wilderness	298	J. Nelson Darby	109
Thou art coming	288	Frances R. Havergal	181
Thou art the everlasting Word	352	Josiah Condor	95
Thou hidden love of God	290	Gerhard Tersteegen	369
Thou my everlasting portion	294	Frances van Alystyne	11
Thou who didst come to die	456	K.H. Elders	129
Thou whose almighty word	457	John Marriott	237
Though often here we're weary	292	Anonymous	13
Through the dark path	293	Mary Carter	79
Through the love of God	296	Mary Peters	295
Through Thy precious body	289	Elizabeth Dark	111
Thy broken body, gracious Lord	291	S.P. Tregelles	381
Thy life was given for me	458	Frances R. Havergal	181
Thy love we own	295	William Yerbury	433
Thy Name we bless	287	S.P. Tregelles	381
Till He come, O let the words	299	E.H. Bickersteth	49
Tis finished, all our souls to win	303	Sir Edward Denny	117
Tis past, the dark and dreary night	304	Sir Edward Denny	117
Tis the blessed hour of prayer	302	Frances van Alystyne	11
Tis we, O Lord, whom Thou	300	Mary Peters	295
To Calvary, Lord, in spirit now	305	Sir Edward Denny	117
To Thee, O gracious Saviour	301	John S.B. Monsell	255
Twas love that sought	297	William Dickinson	123
Twas on that night, when	459	John Morison	261
Unto Him who loved us	307	Samuel W. Waring	395
Unto the Lamb that once was slain	308	Isaac Watts	399
Unworthy our thanksgiving	306	Mary Peters	295
Walk in the light	309	Bernard Barton	25
We bless our Saviour's Name	310	James G. Deck	115
We bless Thee, God our Father	460	Alex. Carruthers	7

First line	No. in B.H.B.	Authors	Page
We come, our gracious Father	311	Anonymous	13
We love to sing with one accord	312	Anonymous	13
We praise Thy great love	313	William P. Mackay	277
We saw Thee not when Thou	461	John H. Gurney	171
We sing the praise of Him	315	Thomas Kelly	211
We'll sing of the Shepherd	318	Thomas Kelly	211
We're a pilgrim band	314	A.B. Mackay	251
What a Friend we have in Jesus	317	Joseph Scriven	327
What grace, O Lord, and beauty	316	Sir Edward Denny	117
What was it, O our God	354	Anne Gilbert	159
What will it be to dwell above	355	Joseph Swain	365
When first o'erwhelmed with	319	James G. Deck	115
When I survey the wondrous Cross	322	Isaac Watts	399
When languor and disease	320	A.M. Toplady	379
When peace, like a river	324	H.G. Spafford	341
When this passing world is done	356	Robt. M. McCheyne	273
When we reach our peaceful	353	Ann Ross Cousin	97
While in sweet communion	323	Sir Edward Denny	117
With Jesus in our midst	325	R.C. Chapman	85
With joy we meditate	320	Isaac Watts	399
With steady pace	331	Anonymous	13
Without a cloud between	351	Albert Midlane	247
Worthy of homage and of praise	462	Fanny T. Wigram	419
Worthy, worthy is the Lamb	328	William P. Mackay	277
Ye gates, lift up your heads	463	Francis Rous & W. Barton	27
Ye servants of God	464	Charles Wesley	403